MILDREDS

THE COOKBOOK

MILDREDS

THE COOKBOOK

DELICIOUS VEGETARIAN RECIPES
FOR SIMPLY EVERYONE

PHOTOGRAPHY BY JONATHAN GREGSON

MITCHELL BEAZLEY

This book is dedicated to everyone who has been involved in Mildreds – you all helped make it what it is today.

'When baking, follow instructions; when cooking, go by your own taste.'
LAIKO BAHRS

An Hachette UK Company
www.hachette.co.uk

First published in Great Britain in 2015 by
Mitchell Beazley, a division of Octopus Publishing Group Ltd,
Carmelite House, 50 Victoria Embankment,
London EC4Y 0DZ

www.octopusbooks.co.uk

Design & layout copyright © Octopus Publishing Group Ltd 2015
Text copyright © Mildreds Limited 2015
Photography copyright © Jonathan Gregson 2015

ISBN 978-1-84533-998-2

A CIP catalogue record for this book is available from the British Library.

Printed and bound in China.

10 9 8 7 6 5 4 3 2 1

Recipe Writers: Daniel Acevedo & Sarah Wasserman
Commissioning Editor: Eleanor Maxfield
Senior Editor: Leanne Bryan
Copy Editor: Simon Davis
Proofreader: Clare Sayer
Indexer: Helen Snaith
Deputy Art Director: Yasia Williams-Leedham
Designer: Patrick Budge
Illustrator: Kirsti-Lee Poulter
Photographer: Jonathan Gregson
Home Economist: Annie Rigg
Prop Stylist & Art Director: Tabitha Hawkins
Assistant Production Manager: Caroline Alberti

CONTENTS

INTRODUCTION

In 1988, when London's Soho was still edgy, Diane Thomas and I took the plunge and opened Mildreds on Greek Street, right in the heart of the West End.

Back then, vegetarian restaurants still had that sixties hippy vibe – doling out 'worthy' brown food into earthenware pottery placed on pine tables. The whole thing felt dated, or so it seemed to us. Our aim was to open a restaurant serving good value, fresh and colourful international vegetarian food. Armed with the supreme confidence of youth (and little else) we took the lease on a small café that, in its former life, had been a seedy sex club... complete with an S&M padded cell in the basement!

At that time our porn baron landlords would come to collect their extortionate rent in person, usually with a glamorous brunette or blonde – wrapped in fur and wearing large, dangly earrings – in tow. After invariably asking for a bacon sandwich, they would slip the envelopes of readies into the inside pockets of their cashmere coats and head out for a 'real meal', as they put it.

The word on the street was that we would last six months.

Yet, despite the prophecies, it turned out that there were people out there who did want to eat the sort of food we were cooking, and we soon became a popular fixture in Soho. With main courses priced at £2.95, we also pretty quickly figured out that we needed to turn those tables to cover the overheads, and so we made the unusual decision (at that time) to take no bookings. As our clientele had nowhere to queue, we would spend a good part of each night running to and fro across the road to the pub, shouting out the names of waiting customers above the pumping rock music.

After 12 years, the opportunity to move to a larger premises – with a proper kitchen, a bar and a private dining room – arose. From inauspicious beginnings, Mildreds had grown up.

Diane Thomas sadly passed away in 2001 but is with us in spirit always.

Many people ask how the name 'Mildreds' came about. I had been waitressing at the impossibly cool 192 before opening the restaurant and wanted a name that stood on its own without reference to wholefoods or vegetarianism. A friend started calling me 'Mildred' after the lead character from the great film noir *Mildred Pierce* starring Joan Crawford. For those who don't know, she was a downtrodden waitress who managed to open a chain of successful restaurants despite being hampered by a scheming social-climbing daughter and a double-crossing playboy lover. The name seemed perfect.

Obviously the food, the service, the ambience and the profit margins are important, but that's only a small part of running a restaurant. There's more. The people who bring the place alive are the staff.

The past 26 years have gone by in the blink of an eye and during that time we have had our fair share of ups and downs. There has been the joy of birth, and the sadness of death and illness. We have risen again after fire, flood and pestilence (the less said about the latter, the better). We have fallen in love, built lasting friendships, suffered breakups and divorce, and weathered recessions (it's been touch and go at times). Yet through it all we've forged ahead together with pride, ambition, ideas, hopes, dreams, laughs and drama (the notorious incident of the missing chef found slumped in the walk-in fridge comes to mind!). We've worked hard to still be here, and now it's better than ever, with more to come. I embrace it all. It's my life. It's what makes me tick.

We still have the same values, integrity and love for what we do that we've had from the very start. Although over the years the food scene has changed, a lot of these changes – such as the move towards using independent suppliers and organic, ethically sourced produce – reflect the way we have always done things.

Daniel, the head chef, and Sarah, our chef extraordinaire, have been the backbone of the Mildreds team for the past ten years. What follows is the culmination of their hard work and talent. They are the real heros of this book.

This book has been a long time coming. We hope you enjoy it.

JANE MUIR

DANIEL ACEVEDO

I always knew I wanted to be a chef. When I was young, I loved being in the kitchen. I remember coming home from school, grabbing my mother's copy of Cookery the Australian Way and baking Anzac biscuits and scones. I must have been about nine or ten years old at the time.

I started professional cookery in 1997 at the age of 17 and trained in various restaurants in and around Melbourne, working mainly with Italian, Greek and pan-Asian cuisines, before deciding in 2005 to move to London to expand my knowledge and further my career as a chef. One of the first jobs that I applied for was at Mildreds. I had never worked in a vegetarian restaurant and jumped at the chance to work somewhere where there would be a strong emphasis on the use of herbs and spices (which has always been the most exciting part of cookery for me).

Over the next couple of years I moved up to the sous chef position within the kitchen and soon after that I took over as head chef.

Working at Mildreds has given – and keeps on giving me – new opportunities, both personally and professionally. I love my job and my team of chefs in the kitchen and would like to thank them for the hard work they have put in over the years I have been nagging, pushing and encouraging them to deliver the best of themselves into the food we make at the restaurant. It simply wouldn't be possible to do what we do without such a strong team.

In October 2010, fellow chef Sarah Wasserman and I started a food blog for Mildreds, primarily with the aim of giving us a platform to experiment and share some of our recipes and daily specials from the restaurant with the blogging community. We always felt, though, that this vegetarian institution deserved a cookbook in its own right, and our blog turned out to be a first step on the road towards accomplishing this.

Many of the restaurant's best-known dishes are featured in this book, along with my favourites, and I love and am very proud of the variety of internationally inspired recipes we have created. Working with Sarah is always a joy and I feel we have really pushed each other to achieve a wonderful book for the restaurant. What a great food adventure it has been!

SARAH WASSERMAN

I have always worked with food, from my first job in a health food store deli in North Carolina, to my time spent hitchhiking across America and my return to London and employment in an eclectic range of busy restaurants. Having misspent my youth at various wonderful London Art colleges, I'm lucky that I had this equal passion, which, unlike my art education, meant I could always put bread on the table!

During my postgrad at the Royal Academy of Art, I would often pass Mildreds and always thought it would be a lovely place to work. Daniel and I started at Mildreds a few days apart and have been friends and collaborators ever since. We started the Mildreds blog together – coming up with recipes, interviewing suppliers and photographing the food in our spare time – so when we got the chance to write the book we jumped at it. I've read cookbooks for fun since primary school and have in the past been known to lug a hardback copy of Claudia Roden's Jewish Food around for a month to read on the Tube. The idea of writing a book of our own was wonderful.

Even though we are sometimes insanely busy at Mildreds, we never rest on our laurels. Jane is always looking for ways in which we can improve, and that drives us as chefs to keep looking for new dishes. The menu is international because we find it really helpful to look to other cultures for vegetarian inspiration. Asian recipes are great for vegan ideas as they contain little or no dairy; the Middle East is good for salads and side dishes as foods from that region are often meat-free; Passover recipes can be excellent for gluten-free ideas, while of course India is a fantastic source of vegetarian food. There is always a new avenue to explore, which is what makes cooking vegetarian food so interesting.

One of the things I like about working at Mildreds is that, although we cater for a wide range of vegetarian diets, nothing is on the menu simply because it fits a particular dietary choice – everything is there on merit. So, if we put a new brownie on the menu it's because we think it's a brilliant brownie. The fact that it's gluten-free and vegan just happens to be the icing on the cake... if you'll forgive the expression.

MILDREDS
AT HOME

 VEGAN

 GLUTEN-FREE

HOW TO USE THIS BOOK

People who choose a vegetarian restaurant may do so for any number of reasons – be they moral, religious, dietary, environmental or just for a change. Nowadays, vegetarian cookery really is for everyone, whether you still enjoy tucking into a steak, or prefer a completely vegetarian diet. Vegetables, fruit, pulses, nuts and seeds have finally taken their rightful place in the kitchen and have stolen the limelight.

Although this book is organized by course, you'll find a number of dishes that can be beefed up to become a main meal or combined with other dishes to share. Look out for notes at the end of some recipes giving tips for dietary requirements, creative variations, flavour twists or recommendations for dishes that go particularly well together.

You'll also find stamps at the top of many of the recipes to flag dishes that are vegan and gluten-free, like the ones on the left. Of course, recipes can also be amended to suit your particular diet. For example, if you want to cook a gluten-free pasta dish, just choose gluten-free pasta instead of the regular kind. Likewise, gluten-free flour can be substituted for regular flour in most instances. Gluten-free vegetable bouillon powder is also a must for gluten-free options.

A NOTE ON COOKING FOR FRIENDS

If only *all* you had to fret about when throwing a dinner party was to pull off a meal that left your satisfied guests begging for your recipes. These days you are also likely to be catering for people with specific dietary preferences, including vegetarians, vegans and guests who are wheat intolerant. Your meal should be full of dishes that everyone can enjoy. Putting a different plate of food in front of someone who can't eat the same as the other guests will only give them the feeling that they have inconvenienced you.

For that reason, there are also some great ideas for gluten-free and vegan dinner menus at the back of the book (*see* pages 244–5 and 246–7). We've also included Middle Eastern mezze and Latin features in the book (*see* pages 60–79 and 158–79), which should give you tons of ideas about what dishes go together.

SOUPS

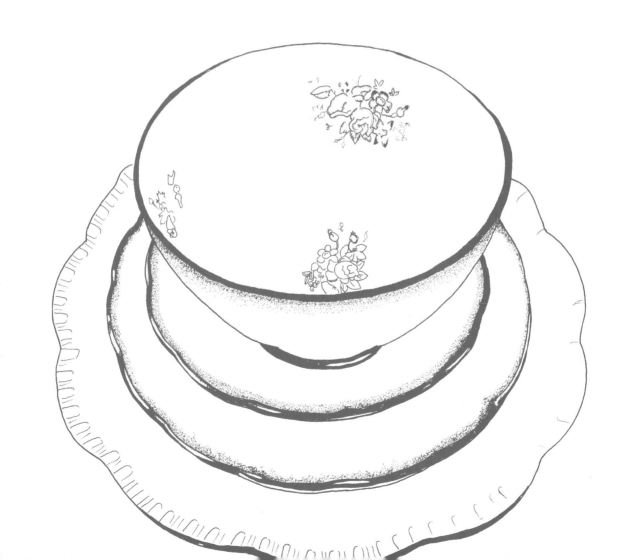

In this rich, creamy and colourful soup the subtle flavour of the lime leaves complements the sweet potato nicely. We use fresh lime leaves when we cook this in the restaurant, but if you're having trouble getting hold of these the dried ones are fine too – just give them a soak in warm water for a few minutes to rehydrate them before using.

THAI-SPICED ROASTED RED PEPPER, SWEET POTATO, GINGER & COCONUT MILK SOUP

SERVES 4–5

6 lime leaves
olive oil
1 small white onion, diced
1 red chilli, trimmed and diced
3 garlic cloves, chopped
3.5-cm (1½-inch) piece of fresh root
  ginger, peeled and chopped
800g (1lb 10oz) sweet potato, peeled
  and cut into 5-cm (2-inch) chunks
2 x 400ml (14fl oz) cans coconut milk
200ml (7fl oz) water
200g (7oz) roasted piquillo peppers
  or other roasted red peppers in oil,
  drained and chopped
salt and pepper
hunks of crusty bread, to serve
  (optional)

Cut out the tough central veins from the lime leaves and discard. Finely slice the remaining lime leaves. Set aside.

Heat a splash of oil in a large saucepan set over a medium heat. Add the onion, chilli, garlic and ginger and cook, stirring, for 8–10 minutes until the onion softens and starts to colour. Add the lime leaf slices and sweet potato chunks and sauté for a further 2–3 minutes.

Pour over the coconut milk and water, stir in the piquillo peppers and bring to a simmer. Leave to cook for 30 minutes, until the sweet potato chunks are soft. At this stage you can add some more water to achieve your desired soup consistency, and check the seasoning to see if salt or pepper is needed.

Purée the soup in a food processor or with a stick blender until smooth and creamy. Serve with hunks of crusty bread, if you like.

This soup makes a nice starter before a noodle-based main, such as **Mee Goreng** (*see* page 156) or **Tempura Vegetables with Noodle, Mango & Cucumber Salad and Chilli Dipping Sauce** (*see* page 56).

If you can't find fresh or dried lime leaves, just add an extra squeeze of **lime juice** and some **fresh coriander** before blending.

If roasted piquillo peppers prove elusive, just roast some **fresh red peppers** instead (*see* page 66).

This is a lovely fresh soup for spring. Blending in the fresh herbs gives it a vibrant green colour which contrasts nicely with the bright yellow rice. The mascarpone can be omitted, or replaced with soy cream, to make this vegan.

MINESTRONE VERDE WITH SAFFRON ARBORIO RICE

SERVES 6–8

olive oil
1 white onion, diced
3 garlic cloves, finely chopped
1 teaspoon fennel seeds, toasted
  and crushed
2 small leeks, trimmed, cleaned and
  finely diced
1 fennel bulb, trimmed and finely diced
100ml (3½fl oz) white wine
750ml–1 litre (1¼–1¾ pints)
  vegetable stock
200g (7oz) baby garden peas
1 courgette, finely diced
100g (3½oz) French beans, trimmed
  and finely chopped
1 bunch of basil
1 bunch of mint
grated rind of ½ lemon
salt and pepper

For the Saffron Arborio Rice
500ml (17fl oz) vegetable stock
small pinch of saffron threads
olive oil
200g (7oz) arborio rice
150ml (¼ pint) white wine

To serve
6–8 teaspoons mascarpone cheese
breadsticks (optional)

For the rice, bring the stock to a simmer in a saucepan, add the saffron and leave to infuse. Heat a splash of oil in a separate saucepan, add the rice and cook, stirring, for a minute. Pour in the wine and let it bubble to reduce down until the pan is quite dry. Gradually add the stock a ladleful at a time, stirring frequently, until the rice is cooked but still firm.

Meanwhile, heat a separate large saucepan with a splash of oil. Add the onion and garlic and cook, stirring, for a few minutes until the onion is translucent. Add the fennel seeds, leeks and fennel bulb and cook, stirring frequently, for 5 minutes until the vegetables soften. Add the wine and reduce until almost evaporated. Pour in the stock and bring to a simmer. Finally add the peas, courgette and beans and simmer for 2–3 minutes.

Remove 500ml (17fl oz) of the soup and blend together with the herbs and grated lemon rind in a food processor or in a bowl with a stick blender until smooth. Pour the mixture back into the soup, stir and adjust the seasoning to taste. Add the rice and heat through.

Ladle the hot soup into bowls, adding a spoonful of mascarpone to the centre of each. Serve immediately, with breadsticks if liked.

A surprisingly creamy soup with a smoky chilli flavour, this is a real favourite among the staff at Mildreds. The pico de gallo (or tomato salsa) adds a nice fresh finish and a splash of colour.

BORLOTTI BEAN SOUP WITH SMOKED TOFU & PICO DE GALLO

SERVES 6–8

olive oil
1 onion, diced
1 red chilli, trimmed, deseeded and
 finely diced
3 garlic cloves, finely chopped
1 celery stick, trimmed and peeled
1 carrot, diced
1 leek, trimmed, cleaned and diced
2 thyme sprigs
1 tablespoon smoked paprika
1 tablespoon ground coriander
2 x 400g (13oz) cans borlotti beans,
 drained and rinsed
1 teaspoon brown sugar
grated rind and juice of ½ lime
1 litre (1¾ pints) water
225g (7½ oz) smoked tofu
salt and pepper

For the pico de gallo
1 chilli, trimmed
4 spring onions, trimmed
handful of coriander leaves
2 tomatoes, flesh and seeds removed
 and reserved for the soup
grated rind and juice of 1 lime

Heat a splash of oil in a large saucepan set over a medium heat. Add the onion and cook, stirring, for 8–10 minutes until soft and translucent, then add the chilli and garlic and cook for another 2 minutes. Add the celery, carrot, leek, thyme and the reserved tomato flesh and seeds from the *pico de gallo* and cook, stirring, over a low heat for 5 minutes until the vegetables start to soften. Add the paprika and ground coriander and sauté for a further 2 minutes to allow the flavours to infuse.

Tip in three-quarters of the borlotti beans, the sugar and grated lime rind and juice. Pour over the water and bring to a simmer. Cook, stirring regularly, for 20 minutes until the beans are beginning to break down.

While the beans are cooking, make the *pico de gallo*. Finely chop the chilli, spring onions, coriander and tomato skins, put in a bowl and mix together with the lime juice and grated rind. Taste and adjust the seasoning if necessary.

Purée the soup in a food processor or with a stick blender until smooth and creamy. Return to the pan, add the remaining beans and the smoked tofu and warm through over a gentle heat. Season with salt and pepper to taste.

Ladle into bowls and serve topped with a spoonful of *pico de gallo*.

This Korean-inspired dish is really more of a broth than a soup, and can be bulked up further with the addition of some cooked noodles or vegetable dumplings if you'd like to serve it as a main course. Although the recipe calls for Korean chilli powder, regular chilli powder works fine too, while if you like a tangy finish, just add a little more tamarind paste.

KOREAN HOT & SOUR SOUP

SERVES 6–8

light oil (such as rapeseed, groundnut
  or sunflower)
1 onion, diced
4 garlic cloves, finely chopped
2.5-cm (1-inch) piece of fresh root
  ginger, peeled and finely chopped
1 red chilli, trimmed and finely sliced
2 teaspoons Korean chilli powder
2 litres (3½ pints) vegetable stock
400g (13oz) can chopped tomatoes
5 tablespoons tamarind paste
2 tablespoons caster sugar
½ Chinese leaf cabbage, shredded
200g (7oz) pak choi, shredded

To garnish
100g (3½ oz) bean sprouts
4 spring onions, finely sliced
handful of coriander sprigs

In a large saucepan, heat a splash of oil and sauté the onion, garlic, ginger and chilli for 5–8 minutes until the onion is translucent. Add the chilli powder and cook, stirring, for another minute or so, then add the vegetable stock, tomatoes, tamarind paste and sugar. Bring to the boil, reduce the heat and simmer for 15–20 minutes to allow the flavours to meld together.

When the broth is cooked, increase the heat, stir in the cabbage and pak choi and cook for 2–3 minutes until tender. Ladle into bowls and garnish with the bean sprouts, spring onion and coriander. Serve.

This tangy Thai soup is absolutely delicious and so good for colds it should be prescribed as medicine. We usually make it with chestnut mushrooms, but button or oyster mushrooms would work equally well. If you can't get hold of palm sugar, just use dark brown sugar instead.

TOMATO & MUSHROOM TOM YUM

SERVES 6–8

7 tomatoes, cut into quarters
sesame oil or other light cooking oil
  (such as rapeseed, groundnut or
  sunflower)
1 white onion, roughly chopped
3 garlic cloves, roughly chopped
2 bird's eye chillies, trimmed and
  roughly chopped
6-cm (2½-inch) piece of peeled fresh
  root galangal or ginger, roughly
  chopped
3 lemon grass stalks, bashed with
  a rolling pin and cut into 3.5-cm
  (1½-inch) pieces
1 bunch of coriander, leaves and
  stalks separated
10 lime leaves
2 tablespoons tamarind paste
70g (2¾oz) palm sugar or dark
  brown sugar
2 tablespoons tomato purée
2 litres (3½ pints) vegetable stock
500g (1lb) chestnut mushrooms,
  trimmed and halved
juice of 2 limes
salt and pepper

Using a spoon, scrape the seeds from the tomato quarters. Set the seeds aside and roughly chop the flesh.

Warm a splash of sesame oil in a large saucepan. Add the onion, garlic, chillies and galangal or ginger to the pan and cook, stirring, for 2–3 minutes until the onion has softened slightly. Add the lemon grass pieces, reserved tomato seeds, coriander stalks and lime leaves and sauté for 5 minutes, until fragrant.

Add the tamarind paste, sugar and tomato purée to the pan and give everything a good stir before adding the stock. Bring to the boil then reduce the heat and simmer gently for at least 20 minutes to allow the flavours to infuse. Season to taste with salt and pepper.

In another saucepan, heat a splash of oil over a medium heat, add the mushrooms and cook until just tender.

Strain the broth through a sieve, add the cooked mushrooms, chopped tomato flesh, coriander leaves and lime juice and ladle into bowls. Serve immediately.

With its ribbons of red cabbage and generous chunks of vegetable and apple, this sweet and sour eastern European classic is almost more of a stew than a broth. Serve it with some delicious rye bread for a hearty winter's lunch. The soured cream can be omitted, or replaced with soy cream, to make this vegan.

BEETROOT, APPLE & RED CABBAGE BORSCHT

SERVES 6–8

2 celery sticks, trimmed
1 carrot, peeled
1 white potato, peeled
1 leek, trimmed and cleaned
2 large beetroot, peeled
1 dessert apple, peeled and cored
light oil (such as rapeseed, groundnut or sunflower)
1 large white onion, finely diced
½ red chilli, trimmed and finely chopped
2.5-cm (1-inch) piece of fresh root ginger, finely chopped
5 garlic cloves, finely chopped
1 teaspoon ground fennel seeds
1 teaspoon ground caraway seeds
200g (7oz) red cabbage, sliced lengthways into 3-mm (⅛-inch) strands
2 star anise
3 tablespoons tomato purée
2 tablespoons balsamic vinegar
750ml (1¼ pints) apple juice
1 litre (1¾ pints) vegetable stock
salt and white pepper

To serve
1 bunch of dill leaves, chopped
6–8 teaspoons soured cream

Cut the celery, carrot, potato, leek, beetroot and apple into 1-cm (½-inch) cubes.

Add a splash of oil to a large saucepan over a medium heat, add the onion and sauté for 5–8 minutes, until it is clear and translucent. Add the chilli, ginger and garlic to the pan and sauté for 2 minutes, then add the carrot, leek, beetroot, ground fennel and caraway seeds and cook, stirring, for a further 15 minutes, until the beetroot is beginning to lose its bite.

Add the red cabbage and cook, stirring, for 2–3 minutes, until the cabbage has begun to soften, then add the star anise, tomato purée and balsamic vinegar along with the cubed celery, potato and apple. Pour over the apple juice and stock, bring to a simmer and cook gently for 45 minutes, until the beetroot pieces are cooked through. Season to taste with salt and pepper.

Ladle the soup into bowls, scatter over the dill leaves and serve with the soured cream alongside for dolloping on top of each serving.

This simple winter soup is all about its three main ingredients, so it's important to get the best quality you can. We use fantastic Spanish haricot beans and they really are worth seeking out for the smooth creamy texture they impart. A dense, sweet variety of pumpkin is perfect for this soup – if all you can find are the more watery varieties then use a butternut squash instead.

PUMPKIN, CAVOLO NERO
& HARICOT BEAN BROTH

SERVES 6–8

olive oil
900g (1¾lb) pumpkin or butternut
  squash, peeled and cut into 2.5-cm
  (1-inch) cubes
1 white onion, finely diced
2.5-cm (1-inch) piece of fresh root
  ginger, peeled and chopped
3 garlic cloves, chopped
3 celery sticks, peeled and very
  finely diced
1 leek, trimmed, cleaned and
  finely diced
1 tablespoon chopped rosemary
1 tablespoon chopped thyme
300ml (½ pint) white wine
2 teaspoons white sugar
2 litres (3½ pints) vegetable stock
475g (15oz) canned haricot beans,
  drained and rinsed
1 head of cavolo nero, stalks removed
  and chopped into bite-sized pieces
salt

Preheat the oven to 190°C/fan 170°C/Gas Mark 5.

Drizzle a little oil on to the base of a roasting tin. Add the pumpkin pieces, season with salt and mix together thoroughly. Roast for 15 minutes, until cooked through. Set aside.

Heat a splash of oil in a large saucepan over a low heat, add the onion, ginger and garlic and cook gently, stirring, for 8 minutes until the onion has begun to soften. Add the celery, leek and herbs and cook, stirring, for another 2 minutes, then add the wine and sugar and simmer for 15–20 minutes until the liquid has reduced by two-thirds.

Pour over the stock, bring to the boil, then reduce to a simmer and cook for 10 minutes, stirring occasionally. Add the beans and simmer for another 10 minutes until the flavours have melded together. Stir in the roasted pumpkin and cavolo nero and simmer for another 2–3 minutes until the cavolo nero is tender. Remove from the heat, ladle into bowls and serve.

A great soup for beating the heat on a summer's day, which has been given a slight twist on the usual with the addition of chopped coriander. To enjoy it at its refreshing best, be sure to let the soup cool down sufficiently before serving. And if the day is really hot, try popping a few ice cubes in each bowl to chill it further still.

GAZPACHO

SERVES 4–6

3 x 400g (13oz) cans chopped tomatoes
100ml (3½fl oz) light olive oil
1 small red onion, finely diced
1 small red pepper, cored, deseeded and
  finely diced
1 small yellow pepper, cored, deseeded
  and finely diced
handful of coriander, leaves picked
  and chopped
1 small cucumber, peeled, deseeded and
  finely diced
2 celery sticks, trimmed and finely diced
450ml (¾ pint) water
3 tablespoons Henderson's Relish or
  vegetarian Worcestershire sauce
4 garlic cloves, very finely chopped
salt and pepper

Tip the tomatoes into a food processor with the olive oil and blend together until smooth, or place in a bowl and use a stick blender. Pass the mixture through a sieve to remove the seeds.

Put the diced onion, peppers, coriander, cucumber, celery and puréed tomato mixture in a large container, add the water, relish and garlic and season to taste with salt and pepper. Stir together well.

Transfer to the refrigerator and leave to chill for at least 1 hour to allow the flavours to develop. Check the seasoning and adjust if necessary before serving.

STARTERS

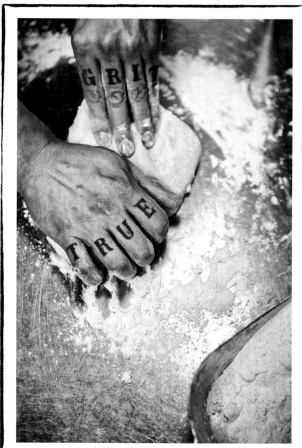

Arancini are a great way to use up leftover risotto. They are lovely served with lemon wedges for squeezing over, though here they are partnered with a warm grilled aubergine and courgette salad for something more substantial. The balsamic pickled onions in this salad can be found in most supermarkets, but if you're struggling to find them then use regular pickled onions instead. To make this recipe gluten-free, simply coat the arancini with gluten-free breadcrumbs.

SUN-BLUSHED TOMATO & MOZZARELLA ARANCINI WITH WARM GRILLED AUBERGINE & COURGETTE SALAD

SERVES 8

1 litre (1¾ pints) vegetable stock
olive oil
1 onion, diced
6 garlic cloves, crushed
150g (5oz) sun-blushed tomatoes in oil, drained and roughly chopped
1 teaspoon dried basil
400g (13oz) arborio rice
handful of fresh basil leaves, chopped
200g (7oz) bocconcini cheese
250g (8oz) dried breadcrumbs
lemon wedges, to serve

For the Warm Grilled Aubergine & Courgette Salad
4 courgettes, cut into 1-cm (½-inch) diagonal slices
2 large aubergines, cut into 1.5cm (¾ inch) round discs
60ml (2½fl oz) light olive oil
2 garlic cloves, finely chopped
8 balsamic pickled onions, cut into quarters, plus 2 tablespoons of juice
handful of flat leaf parsley leaves, chopped
2 tablespoons extra virgin olive oil
1 tablespoon good-quality aged balsamic vinegar or balsamic glaze
sea salt flakes

Bring the stock to a simmer in a saucepan. Heat a splash of oil in a separate saucepan, add the onion and garlic and cook, stirring, for 2–3 minutes or until the onion has started to soften. Add the tomatoes, dried basil and rice and sauté for a further 2 minutes.

Gradually add the stock to the rice a ladleful at a time, stirring frequently, until the rice is cooked but still firm. Remove from the heat and transfer to a small tray or large plate and leave to cool for 10 minutes, then refrigerate for a further 15–20 minutes.

Meanwhile, make the salad. Heat a griddle pan or large heavy-based frying pan over a medium heat. Mix the courgette and aubergine slices with the oil and garlic in a mixing bowl, add to the pan, and cook until tender; about 1–2 minutes on each side for the courgettes and at least 2–3 minutes on each side for the aubergines. Remove from the heat and return to the bowl with the pickled onions, pickling juice, chopped parsley, extra virgin olive oil and balsamic vinegar. Season with sea salt flakes and mix together well. Set aside.

Remove the cooled rice from the refrigerator, add the chopped fresh basil to the rice and mix together well. Shape into 4-cm (1¾-inch) balls, pushing a piece of bocconcini into the centre of each with your thumb. Roll the *arancini* in the breadcrumbs. Heat a thin layer of oil in a frying pan. Add the *arancini* and fry for 2–3 minutes on each side until golden brown. Serve with the warm grilled aubergine and courgette salad, and the lemon wedges, for squeezing over.

Summer rolls have proved to be a very popular addition to our menu. Gluten-free, vegan and very light, they make a great snack on a hot day. They are really simple to make but you may have to go to an Asian supermarket to find the rice paper sheets.

MANGO SUMMER ROLLS WITH SPICY PEANUT SAUCE

SERVES 4–6

90g (3oz) vermicelli rice noodles
100g (3½oz) bean sprouts
1 large red chilli, trimmed and diced
grated rind of 2 limes
12 x 22cm (9 inch) rice paper wrappers
½ cucumber, deseeded and cut into
 5-mm- (¼-inch-) thick batons
1 small ripe mango, peeled and cut
 into 5-mm- (¼-inch-) thick batons
handful of mint, leaves picked
handful of fresh coriander, leaves
 picked, plus extra to garnish
1 medium beetroot, coarsely grated
1 large carrot, coarsely grated

For the Spicy Peanut Sauce
200g (7oz) crunchy peanut butter
200ml (7fl oz) water
1 red chilli, trimmed and finely diced
juice of 2 limes
1 tablespoon dark muscovado sugar
4 garlic cloves, very finely chopped
1.5-cm (¾-inch) piece of fresh root
 ginger, peeled and very finely
 chopped

Cook or soak the rice noodles in boiling water according to the packet instructions, then drain well and leave to cool. Once cool, tip into a bowl with the bean sprouts, chilli and grated lime rind and mix together well.

Wet a rice paper wrapper by dipping it in a bowl of water for 15–20 seconds until it starts to soften and become pliable, then place it on a clean work surface. Arrange a few batons of cucumber and mango across the centre of the wrapper, leaving a gap of 4–5cm (1½–2 inches) either side for folding. Add a few mint and coriander leaves, then a small handful of the noodle mix and grated vegetables.

Bring the bottom and top edges of the wrapper tightly up over the filling then fold the sides in over it. Continue to roll up tightly and place on a plate. Repeat this process with the remaining rolls and filling ingredients.

To make the spicy peanut sauce, put all the ingredients in a bowl and whisk together until smooth.

Serve the rolls accompanied by the spicy peanut sauce and garnished with coriander leaves

What more can we say? When asparagus comes into season for those short few weeks in late spring and early summer there's nothing better to eat – particularly when paired with freshly poached eggs and a generous serving of hollandaise sauce. In this hollandaise we have used orange juice instead of lemon juice to give it a sweeter, fruitier tang.

ROASTED ASPARAGUS WITH POACHED EGGS & ORANGE HOLLANDAISE

SERVES 4–6

16 asparagus spears
sea salt flakes
4 tablespoons olive oil
25ml (1fl oz) cider or white wine vinegar
4–6 eggs

For the Orange Hollandaise
2 egg yolks
1 tablespoon cider vinegar
500g (1lb) butter, melted
juice of ½ small orange
salt and pepper

Preheat the oven to 190°C/fan 170°C/Gas Mark 5. Line a baking tray with baking parchment.

To prepare the asparagus, snap off the woody base of the stalks. Lay the asparagus on the prepared baking tray, sprinkle with sea salt flakes and drizzle over the olive oil. Roast for 10 minutes until the asparagus spears are tender but still firm.

Meanwhile prepare your hollandaise sauce by whisking the yolks and vinegar in a bowl set over a pan of gently simmering water until the yolks are thick, pale and tripled in volume. Remove from the heat and whisk in three-quarters of the butter, continuing to whisk until the sauce is thick and shiny. Whisk in the orange juice and the remaining butter, leaving out the pale white milk solids that will have formed when the butter melted. Season with salt and pepper and cover with a tea towel to keep warm until needed.

Bring a large saucepan of water to the boil and lower the heat to bring it to a rolling simmer. Add the vinegar and give the water a light clockwise swirl with a spoon. Crack one of the eggs into a cup and pour it into the water. Repeat with the remaining eggs and poach for approximately 2–3 minutes, until the whites are set but the yolks are still soft. Lift out the eggs with a slotted spoon and drain on a clean tea towel.

Divide the asparagus spears between plates, top with the eggs and drizzle over the hollandaise sauce. Garnish with freshly ground black pepper and serve.

These delicious cakes would make a perfect Christmas starter, or a Boxing Day lunch using the leftover roasted vegetables from the big meal itself. The gooey melted rarebit in the centre of the cakes transforms the bubble and squeak into something quite special.

BUBBLE & SQUEAK CAKES
FILLED WITH WELSH RAREBIT

SERVES 6–8

olive oil

1kg (2lb) potatoes, peeled and cut into
   4-cm (1½-inch) chunks

2 carrots, peeled, halved and cut into
   5-cm (2-inch) pieces

2 parsnips, peeled and cut into 4-cm
   (1½-inch) chunks

½ small onion, chopped

300g (10oz) cabbage, chopped

1 rosemary sprig

1 thyme sprig

50g (2oz) peas, defrosted if frozen

5 spring onions, trimmed and finely
   sliced

salt

For the Welsh Rarebit

50g (2oz) butter

3 tablespoons gluten-free plain flour
   (or plain flour, for non gluten-free)

150ml (¼ pint) gluten-free ale
   (or regular ale, for non gluten-free)

250g (8oz) smoked Cheddar or regular
   mature Cheddar cheese

2 teaspoons Dijon mustard

1 teaspoon Henderson's Relish or
   vegetarian Worcestershire sauce

3 tablespoons soured cream

To serve

65g (2½oz) watercress leaves

6–8 tablespoons cranberry sauce

Preheat the oven to 200°C/fan 180°C/Gas Mark 5.

For the rarebit, melt the butter in a saucepan over a low heat, add the flour and cook, stirring, for 1 minute. Add the ale, cheese, mustard, relish and soured cream and cook, stirring, until the cheese has melted and the sauce is thick. Spoon into a container and chill in the freezer for 15–20 minutes, until the rarebit is cold but still pliable. Once chilled, divide the mixture into 12–16 pieces and shape into balls. Flatten slightly to finish. Return to the freezer until needed.

Splash a little oil on to the base of a roasting tin, add the potatoes, carrots and parsnips, season with salt and mix together thoroughly. Roast for 20–25 minutes, until the vegetables are golden brown at the edges. Set aside to cool.

Heat a drizzle of oil in a frying pan, add the onion and sauté for 8–10 minutes until translucent. Add the cabbage and herbs and cook, stirring, for 3–4 minutes until tender. Set aside.

Tip the roasted vegetables into a bowl with the peas and roughly mash together. Add the onion, cabbage and spring onions and mix together with your hands. Take a scoop of the mixture and flatten it in your hand to just bigger than the size of your palm. Place a rarebit ball in the centre and fold the mixture around it to form a cake. Repeat with the remaining bubble and squeak and rarebit balls.

Heat a layer of olive oil in a large nonstick frying pan over a medium heat. Add the potato cakes and fry for 4 minutes on each side until brown and crispy. Serve with watercress and cranberry sauce.

The stunning colours in this simple starter bring summer to the table. If you can't find peaches, nectarines are a good substitute. The trick with this is to serve it straight away while the peaches are still warm so that the labneh softens alongside it. The pomegranate molasses, which can be found in delicatessens and now in some supermarkets, adds a wonderful sweet and sour finish.

Labneh is a delicious, creamy Middle Eastern cheese made with yogurt. If you've never made cheese before don't worry, it couldn't be easier. The recipe makes more than you will need and the cheese is lovely in salad or dolloped on top of stews, tagines or soups. The spices in this recipe are just a suggestion, you can use whatever you prefer.

HOMEMADE LABNEH CHEESE WITH GRILLED PEACHES, ALMONDS, ROCKET & POMEGRANATE MOLASSES

SERVES 6

5 peaches
100g (3½oz) rocket leaves
60g (2½oz) toasted flaked almonds
1 pomegranate, seeds removed
 (optional)
75ml (3fl oz) extra virgin olive oil
75ml (3fl oz) pomegranate molasses

For the Homemade Labneh Cheese
500ml (17fl oz) Greek yogurt
grated rind and juice of 1 lemon
1 garlic clove, finely chopped
1 teaspoon sumac
½ teaspoon chilli flakes
½ teaspoon ground cumin
1½ teaspoons salt

To make the labneh, mix all the ingredients together in a bowl. Cover a sieve with muslin, place it over a separate bowl and pour over the cheese mixture. Tie the opposite ends of the muslin together before tying the ends around a wooden spoon. Suspend above a container deep enough to ensure the cloth clears the bottom by at least 10cm (4 inches). Transfer to the refrigerator and leave to drain for 24–48 hours, depending on your preferred consistency (after 24 hours the cheese will be soft and creamy whereas 48 hours will leave you with a firmer cheese like a full-fat cream cheese).

To make the salad, cut the peaches in half along the seam, twist to open and prise out the stones. Heat a large griddle pan until hot, add the peach halves flesh-side down and cook for around 5 minutes until nicely blackened and charred. Turn them over and cook for 1 minute on the skin side until tender.

Slice each peach half into three pieces and divide among plates with the rocket leaves. Top each with a tablespoon of labneh and scatter over the flaked almonds and pomegranate seeds, if using. Drizzle over the oil and pomegranate molasses and serve immediately.

This very simple starter is perfect for the autumn when figs are at their best. It's one of those great dishes that looks like it takes ages to make but is actually whipped up in minutes. We also like to serve it with homemade Polenta Biscuits (see opposite) and they are well worth putting in the extra effort on those occasions when time is not an issue. The biscuits can be omitted, or replaced with gluten-free crackers, to make this recipe gluten-free.

FIGS WITH BLUE CHEESE
MOUSSE & ROASTED HAZELNUTS

SERVES 4

12 ripe fresh figs
150g (5oz) watercress
55g (2oz) roasted hazelnuts
3 tablespoons extra virgin olive oil
Polenta Biscuits, to serve (*see* opposite)

For the Blue Cheese Mousse
100ml (3½fl oz) double cream
100g (3½oz) blue cheese
100g (3½oz) cream cheese
1 small rosemary sprig, leaves picked
  and roughly chopped
1 teaspoon Dijon mustard
salt and pepper

To make the mousse, lightly whip the double cream in a bowl with a whisk. Roughly dice the blue cheese and add to a food processor along with the cream cheese, rosemary and mustard. Blend until smooth. Remove from the food processor and fold into the cream with a spatula. Season to taste with salt and pepper.

Make two crossways cuts three-quarters of the way down each fig and squeeze the sides to open them up like flowers. Divide between plates with the watercress leaves and serve with a dollop of the mousse, a scattering of roasted hazelnuts and a drizzle of olive oil. Serve with Polenta Biscuits, if desired.

These lovely, crunchy polenta biscuits are great with cheese. We also like to serve them with our Figs with Blue Cheese Mousse & Roasted Hazelnuts starter (see opposite).

POLENTA BISCUITS

MAKES 8–10 BISCUITS

50g (2oz) butter
1 tablespoon caster sugar
75g (3oz) quick-cook polenta
75g (3oz) plain flour, plus extra
  for dusting
40–50ml (1½–2fl oz) water

Beat together the butter and sugar in a mixing bowl until pale and creamy. Add the dry ingredients and mix well, gradually adding the water to form a smooth, firm dough. Shape into a ball, wrap in clingfilm and refrigerate for 15–20 minutes.

Preheat the oven to 190°C/fan 170°C/Gas Mark 5. Line a large baking tray with baking parchment.

Remove the dough from the refrigerator and roll out into a circle on a lightly floured surface to a thickness of 5mm (¹/₄ inch). Slice into 8–10 triangular pieces, as if cutting a cake, and arrange them on the prepared baking tray. Cook for 20–25 minutes until golden brown. Set aside to cool on a wire rack.

For a savoury option, add **fresh thyme** or **rosemary** to the recipe along with some **freshly cracked black pepper**.

The spring vegetables and fresh mint give these pakora a very light, delicate finish that works well with our creamy mango yogurt dip. For a vegan option, substitute plain vegan yogurt in the Mango Yogurt Dip. These are at their best served straight out of the pan while still crisp and hot.

SPRING VEGETABLE PAKORA
WITH MANGO YOGURT DIP

SERVES 4–5

250g (8oz) tenderstem broccoli, trimmed
250g (8oz) fennel bulb, trimmed
½ white onion
100g (3½oz) peas, defrosted if frozen
10 mint leaves
vegetable oil, for deep-frying

For the Mango Yogurt Dip
250g (8oz) mango, peeled and chopped
1 green chilli, trimmed
grated zest of ½ lime plus juice of 1 lime
10 mint leaves
200ml (7fl oz) yogurt

For the batter
250g (8oz) gram flour
50g (2oz) gluten-free self-raising flour (or self-raising flour, for non gluten-free)
1 teaspoon curry powder
1 tablespoon lemon juice
1 green chilli, trimmed and finely chopped

Slice the broccoli spears in half, cut out the tough central cores from the bottom of the fennel and onion bulbs and cut the remainder into 1-cm- (½-inch-) thick slices. Put them in a bowl with the peas and mint leaves and mix together well with your hands.

For the mango yogurt dip, put two-thirds of the mango and all the remaining ingredients into a blender and blend until smooth. Stir in the remaining mango to finish.

Half-fill a large saucepan or deep-fryer with vegetable oil and heat to 180°C (350°F), or until a cube of bread thrown into the oil browns in 30 seconds.

While the oil is heating, make the batter. Combine the gram flour, self-raising flour and curry powder together in a large bowl. Add the lemon juice and green chilli and gradually pour in enough water to give the mixture the consistency of double cream, whisking all the while to remove any lumps.

Take a few small handfuls of the vegetable mix and dip into the batter to coat evenly. Deep-fry the pakora in batches for 5–6 minutes until crisp and golden, then drain on kitchen paper to soak up the excess oil. Serve immediately with the mango yogurt dip.

These surprisingly light and fluffy blinis are filled with sweet potato and coconut, giving them a pleasantly sweet flavour that balances well with the peppery Caribbean spices of the okra and jerk dressing.

SWEET POTATO & COCONUT BLINIS
WITH PAN-FRIED OKRA & JERK DRESSING

SERVES 6–8

2 tablespoons light olive oil or other
 light cooking oil (such as rapeseed,
 groundnut or sunflower), plus extra
 for frying
700g (1½lb) sweet potatoes, peeled and
 cut into 3-cm (1¼-inch) chunks
½ red chilli, trimmed and chopped
40g (1½oz) creamed coconut
200ml (7fl oz) coconut milk
pinch of ground cinnamon
pinch of paprika
50g (2oz) wheat-free plain flour
2 large eggs, separated
500g (1lb) okra, topped and tailed
salt and pepper

For the Jerk Dressing
1 teaspoon coriander seeds
1 allspice berry
1-cm (½-inch) piece of fresh root
 ginger, peeled
2 red chillies, trimmed and chopped
1 bunch of coriander leaves
grated rind and juice of 1 lime
100ml (3½fl oz) light oil (such as
 rapeseed, groundnut or sunflower)
3 garlic cloves

Preheat the oven to 200°C/fan 180°C/Gas Mark 6. Drizzle the oil on to the base of a roasting tin. Add the sweet potato pieces and chopped chilli, season with salt and mix together thoroughly. Roast for 15–20 minutes, until the sweet potato is cooked. Set aside to cool.

Gently warm the creamed coconut in a microwave or a small saucepan over a low heat to soften it, then tip it into a food processor with the sweet potato pieces, coconut milk, cinnamon, paprika and flour. Season to taste with salt and pepper and blend until smooth. Transfer to a large bowl and stir in the egg yolks. Whip the egg whites in a separate bowl until soft peaks form, then carefully fold into the blini mixture.

Warm a splash of oil in a nonstick frying pan over a low heat. Drop spoonfuls of the mix into the pan and cook for 3 minutes on each side until golden brown, turning carefully. Continue until you have used up all the mixture. Keep the fritters warm in a low oven.

For the jerk dressing, toast the coriander seeds and allspice berry in a dry frying pan over a medium heat for a minute until fragrant. Using a pestle and mortar, grind the toasted spices together, then add to a small bowl with the remaining ingredients. Blend everything together using a stick blender or in a food processor to form a thick, spiced oil.

Heat a drizzle of oil in a wok or large frying pan over a medium heat. Put the okra in a sieve and rinse under running water. Tip into the wok and cook, stirring, for about 5 minutes, until the okra has puffed up and softened slightly. Add 2–3 tablespoons of the jerk dressing and cook, stirring, for a further minute, then remove from the heat. Arrange the blini on a serving platter, top with the okra and drizzle the remaining jerk dressing around the plate to finish.

Latkes are eastern European or Russian rösti pancakes that are usually made with potatoes and served with apple sauce. Our recipe borrows a lot of flavours from Indian cooking and this unlikely combination works really well to lighten up what can typically be quite a heavy dish. For best results serve the latkes straight away, fresh from the pan.

SPICED CARROT, APPLE & PARSNIP LATKES
WITH CUCUMBER RIBBON SALAD

SERVES 6–8

3 carrots, peeled
2 parsnips, peeled
1 dessert apple, peeled and cored
2.5-cm (1-inch) piece of fresh root
  ginger, peeled
1 white onion, very finely diced
1 teaspoon coriander seeds
1 teaspoon cumin seeds
½ teaspoon chilli powder
1 teaspoon turmeric powder
2 eggs, lightly beaten
2 tablespoons fine polenta
1 tablespoon gluten-free plain flour
  (or plain flour, for non gluten-free)
light cooking oil (such as rapeseed,
  groundnut or sunflower)
Mango Yogurt Dip (*see* page 49),
  to serve

For the Cucumber Ribbon Salad
2 cucumbers, peeled
1 green chilli, trimmed, deseeded and
  finely chopped
grated rind and juice of 1 lime
8 mint leaves
4 spring onions, trimmed and chopped

Coarsely grate the carrots, parsnips and apple into a mixing bowl. Finely grate the ginger and add to the bowl with the onion. Mix everything together well.

Toast the coriander and cumin seeds in a dry frying pan over a medium heat for about a minute until fragrant. Using a pestle and mortar, grind the toasted spices together with the chilli powder and turmeric. Tip into the bowl with the vegetables, add the beaten egg, polenta and flour and mix together well until evenly combined.

For the cucumber ribbon salad, shave the cucumber into wide ribbons with a vegetable peeler. Combine with the other ingredients in a bowl. Set aside.

Heat a thin layer of oil in a wide frying pan. You will need to fry the latkes in batches: drop several spoonfuls of the mixture into the pan, spacing them apart, and fry for 2–3 minutes on each side until golden and cooked through. Transfer to a warm plate lined with kitchen paper and keep warm while you cook the rest: there should be enough mixture for 6–8 fritters.

Divide the latkes between plates, top with the cucumber salad and serve immediately accompanied by the Mango Yogurt Dip.

This crostini is a very simple starter that has proved perennially popular at Mildreds. To make it work you do need to use good-quality artichokes, though; look for the tender ones with the long stems that are preserved in oil (the ones in vacuum packs rather than cans are worth hunting down as they taste better and are fresher). You can find them in any decent Italian delicatessen or other Mediterranean food store.

ARTICHOKE CROSTINI
WITH ROAST GARLIC & LEMON AIOLI

SERVES 4

8 focaccia or sourdough bread slices
6–8 good-quality artichoke hearts in oil, drained
75g (3oz) mixed baby leaf lettuce
4 tablespoons Roast Garlic & Lemon Aioli (*see* page 234)

Heat a griddle pan or heavy-based frying pan over a high heat. Add the bread slices and toast them for 1^1/$_2$–2 minutes on each side until they are nicely charred.

Slice the artichokes in half lengthways. Add to the pan and griddle for 1–2 minutes on each side. Divide the artichokes, toasted bread slices and lettuce leaves between plates and serve with Roast Garlic & Lemon Aioli.

If you would like to make this vegan, substitute our **Vegan Basil Mayonnaise** (*see* page 232).

This is a nice starter to precede an Italian main such as the **Tenderstem Broccoli & Asparagus White Lasagne** (*see* page 112).

These popular Eastern-European filled pancakes, known as blintzes in the Ashkenazi Jewish community, are often made with fruit as a brunch dish or dessert. This savoury version makes an elegant dinner party starter. Although they may seem a little labour-intensive, everything is very straightforward, while the pancakes can be made up in advance of the final filling and cooking stages. Serve with a lightly dressed green salad.

SAVOURY HAZELNUT PANCAKES FILLED WITH CHANTERELLE MUSHROOMS & MASCARPONE

MAKES 8–10 PANCAKES

100g (3½oz) blanched hazelnuts
100g (3½oz) plain flour
2 eggs
1 tablespoon melted butter, plus extra
  for frying
200ml (7fl oz) milk, plus extra if needed
light oil (such as rapeseed, groundnut
  or sunflower)

For the filling
light oil (such as rapeseed, groundnut
  or sunflower)
1 small onion, finely diced
3 garlic cloves, very finely chopped
1 leek, trimmed, cleaned and finely
  sliced
250g (8oz) chanterelle and/or black
  trumpet mushrooms, trimmed and
  torn into 1-cm (½-inch) strips
1 tablespoon white wine (optional)
grated rind of ½ lemon
300g (10oz) mascarpone cheese or
  cream cheese
handful of chives, chopped

To make the pancake batter, blend the hazelnuts and flour together in a food processor. Add the eggs and melted butter and pulse, adding the milk in a steady stream, until it achieves the consistency of double cream (if it is looking too thick, add a little more milk). Transfer to a bowl, cover with clingfilm and leave to chill in the refrigerator for 20 minutes.

Prepare a frying pan by heating it well and wiping it with oil. Pour in enough batter to thinly coat the bottom of the pan and cook until bubbles begin to form in the centre. Flip the pancake over with a palette knife or spatula and cook the other side until brown. Turn the pancake out on to a plate and make the remaining pancakes. Set aside until needed.

For the filling, heat a splash of oil in a frying pan over a medium heat, add the onion and sauté for 8–10 minutes until translucent. Add the garlic, leek, mushrooms and a splash of white wine, if using, and cook, stirring, for 3–4 minutes, until the mushrooms have softened. Remove from the heat and mix in the grated lemon rind, mascarpone and chives.

Divide the filling mixture evenly between the pancakes. Fold each end and then the sides to meet in the middle to form rectangular parcels. Warm a little butter in a frying pan and fry the filled pancakes for 2–3 minutes on each side until golden brown. Serve immediately.

This is a lovely rustic pie which makes great use of the delicate sweet flesh of autumn pumpkin or squash. It has been on the menu at Mildreds in the past but here we've re-sized it for making at home. We like to keep it a bit messy too, not worrying about trimming the pastry or glazing the top, though if you like a shine on your pie, simply give it a little brush with beaten egg or soy cream before baking.

PUMPKIN, FETA & PIQUILLO PEPPER PIE

SERVES 8–10

2 tablespoons olive oil

1kg (2lb) pumpkin or butternut squash, peeled, deseeded and cut into 2.5-cm (1-inch) chunks

4 small rosemary sprigs, leaves picked and roughly chopped

4 garlic cloves, finely sliced

1 red chilli, trimmed and finely diced

6 roasted piquillo peppers or other roasted red peppers in oil, drained and sliced

200g (7oz) feta cheese

sea salt flakes

For the pastry

400g (13oz) plain flour, plus extra to dust

200g (7oz) butter (cubed and cold)

1 tablespoon chopped fresh herbs (such as oregano, sage or thyme)

1 egg yolk

ice-cold water

Preheat the oven to 190°C/fan 170°C/Gas Mark 5.

For the pastry, place the flour in a bowl, add the butter and rub in with your fingertips until the mixture resembles fine breadcrumbs. Add the herbs, egg yolk and enough ice-cold water to mix a firm dough. Knead together briefly, cover with clingfilm and leave to rest in the refrigerator for 15 minutes.

Meanwhile, prepare your filling. Drizzle the oil on to the base of a roasting tin, add the pumpkin pieces, rosemary, garlic and chilli, season with sea salt flakes and mix together thoroughly. Roast in the oven for 25–30 minutes, until the pumpkin is very soft and almost collapsing on itself. Set aside to cool, then tip into a bowl with the piquillo peppers. Crumble over the feta cheese and mix together well.

Take two-thirds of the pastry and roll it out on a lightly floured surface to a 5-mm (¼-inch) thickness and use to line a 23-cm (9-inch) loose-bottomed tart tin. Spoon the filling evenly over the base of the pie. Roll out the remaining pastry to a 5-mm (¼-inch) thickness and lay it over the top of the pie, folding and crimping the edges to seal.

Bake in the oven for 30–40 minutes until golden brown. Cut into slices and serve.

This is one of our favourite dishes for the warmer months – it's full of lovely fresh flavours and is great when mangoes are at their best. You can use any type of wheat or rice noodle here; just avoid egg noodles as these are best eaten hot.

TEMPURA VEGETABLES WITH NOODLE, MANGO & CUCUMBER SALAD & CHILLI DIPPING SAUCE

SERVES 4–6

For the dressing
100ml (3½fl oz) mirin
juice of 2 limes
2 green chillies, deseeded and finely diced
25ml (1fl oz) Japanese rice vinegar
60ml (2½fl oz) soy sauce
½ teaspoon light muscovado sugar

For the noodles
250g (8oz) soba noodles or rice noodles
light oil
1 cucumber, finely diced
1 mango, peeled and finely diced
1 red chilli, deseeded and chopped
½ small red onion, finely diced
1 bunch of coriander leaves, chopped
handful of mint leaves, chopped

For the Tempura Vegetables
1 litre (1¾ pints) sunflower oil
330ml (11fl oz) ice-cold sparkling water
180g (6oz) plain flour, plus extra
  for dusting
2 eggs
½ teaspoon baking powder
25g (1oz) black sesame seeds, toasted
25g (1oz) white sesame seeds, toasted
2 courgettes, quartered and cut into
  10-cm (4-inch) batons
1 red pepper, cored, deseeded and cut
  into 10-cm (4-inch) batons
1 yellow pepper, cored, deseeded and
  cut into 10-cm (4-inch) batons
2 carrots, thinly sliced

To make the dressing, put all the ingredients in a mixing bowl and mix together well.

Cook the noodles in a pan of boiling water according to the packet instructions. Transfer to a sieve and cool under running water, adding a drop or two of oil to prevent them from sticking together. Tip into a mixing bowl, add the cucumber, mango, chilli, onion, herbs and 50ml (2fl oz) of the dressing and mix together well. Set aside.

For the tempura vegetables, fill a large saucepan or deep-fryer with the sunflower oil and heat to 180°C (350°F), or until a cube of bread thrown into the oil browns in 30 seconds.

Put the sparkling water, flour, eggs, baking powder and sesame seeds in a bowl and whisk together briefly to form a batter (don't overwork this; it's fine if it is slightly lumpy). Working in batches, lightly dust a handful of the vegetables in flour and dip them into the batter. Fry the vegetables for about 3–4 minutes until lightly golden, remove from the pan and turn out on to kitchen paper to drain off the excess oil. Repeat with the remaining vegetables, being sure to remove any excess batter from the pan before frying the next batch.

Serve the tempura vegetables alongside the noodle salad, with the remainder of the dressing in a bowl as a dipping sauce.

If you would like to make this gluten-free, substitute **gluten-free plain flour** for the **regular plain flour** used here. However, note that you may need to use a little more of it to achieve the desired thickness of batter.

This starter is all about textures, with the crispy polenta making a great crunchy contrast to the creamy mascarpone cheese and sharp, juicy tomatoes. Cooked like this, polenta also makes a wonderful side dish for slow-cooked vegetable dishes such as caponata or ratatouille.

CRISPY POLENTA WITH SLOW-ROAST CHERRY TOMATOES & LEMON MASCARPONE

SERVES 6

450g (14½oz) cherry tomatoes,
  preferably on the vine
2 tablespoons olive oil, plus extra
  for oiling
pinch of dried oregano
800ml (1½ pints) vegetable stock
200g (7oz) quick-cook polenta
100ml (3½fl oz) vegetable oil
sea salt flakes

For the Lemon Mascarpone
rind of 1 lemon, finely chopped, plus
  1 tablespoon lemon juice
500g (1lb) mascarpone cheese
salt

To serve
65g (2½oz) rocket leaves
100ml (3½fl oz) Wild Garlic Pesto
  (*see* page 147) or Purple Basil Oil
  (*see* page 238)

Preheat the oven to 110°C/fan 90°C/Gas Mark ¼. Line a baking tray with baking parchment.

Place the tomatoes on the prepared baking tray, drizzle over the olive oil and sprinkle with the oregano and a pinch of sea salt flakes. Bake in the oven for about 2 hours, until the tomatoes have wrinkled, begun to dry out and intensified in flavour.

Meanwhile, prepare the polenta. Pour the stock into a medium saucepan, salt lightly and bring to the boil. Add the polenta and cook, whisking thoroughly to avoid lumps, for 3–4 minutes until the polenta thickens and all the stock has been absorbed.

Tip the polenta on to a lightly oiled 25-cm (10-inch) plate or small tray. Using a spatula, smooth the polenta evenly to a 2.5-cm (1-inch) thickness. Refrigerate for 15–20 minutes to cool and set.

To make the lemon mascarpone, put the lemon rind, lemon juice and mascarpone in a bowl. Season with salt and mix together well.

Heat the vegetable oil in a small frying pan over a medium heat. Cut the polenta into 10-cm (4-inch) triangles, add to the pan and cook for about 2 minutes on each side until golden brown.

To serve, place the polenta slices on plates and top with the rocket and slow-roasted tomatoes. Drizzle over the Wild Garlic Pesto or Purple Basil Oil and garnish with a generous dollop of lemon mascarpone.

MEZZE

Mediterranean and Middle Eastern cuisines are so rich in vegetarian and vegan dishes that we found putting together this banquet of mezze dishes a breeze. In fact, the hard part was knowing where to stop, with so many dishes to choose from, many of them boasting beautiful colours as well as flavours. You may find a few things here that you haven't tried before, or come across some new takes on old favourites. Either way, this collection of small plates is ideal when you want your table to be a feast for the eyes as well as the palate.

Combining gooey cheese with crunchy courgettes, these fritters make for an utterly moreish mouthful and are at their best straight from the pan. Pair them with Harissa (see page 228) and Cucumber Ribbon Salad (see page 51) for a great starter.

HALOUMI, COURGETTE & MINT FRITTERS

SERVES 6–8 AS PART OF A MEZZE PLATTER

240g (8oz) haloumi cheese, coarsely grated
½ red onion, finely diced
1 large chilli, trimmed and finely diced
3 garlic cloves, finely chopped
1 small bunch of mint, finely chopped
grated rind of 1 lemon
2 courgettes, coarsely grated
3 eggs, lightly beaten
100g–150g (3½–5oz) fresh white breadcrumbs
2 tablespoons plain flour, for coating
light cooking oil (such as rapeseed, groundnut or sunflower)

To serve
Harissa (*see* page 228)
lemon wedges

Put the grated haloumi in a bowl with the onion, chilli, garlic, mint and grated lemon rind and mix together well.

Wrap the courgettes in a clean tea towel and squeeze to remove any excess liquid. Tip into the bowl along with the eggs and just enough of the breadcrumbs to hold everything together. Cover with clingfilm and leave to rest in the refrigerator for at least 10 minutes.

Using your hands, shape the mixture into egg-sized patties, adding more breadcrumbs if the mix is very sticky. Toss the fritters lightly in the flour to coat, shaking off any excess.

Warm a splash of oil in a frying pan over a medium heat. Cook the fritters in batches for 2–3 minutes on each side until golden brown. Serve immediately with Harissa, and lemon wedges for squeezing over.

For a gluten-free option, make the **breadcrumbs** with a **gluten-free bread**.

For a main course, serve the fritters wrapped in a **thin flatbread**, accompanied by our **Ruby Jewelled Tabbouleh** (*see* page 96) or our **Wild Rice Salad with Peas, Pea Shoots & Green Harissa** (*see* page 84).

These little flatbreads are often called Turkish pizzas, although they are popular across the Middle East. The name translates as 'meat on dough' in Arabic, so ours is a loose interpretation. We have tried to maintain the richness of the typical topping while adding a little tang with a bit of tomato and tamarind. Another diversion from tradition is that these are party-sized – just make them up at twice the size for a main course. Enjoy them warm, smothered with hummus and salad, or just on their own fresh from the oven.

ROAST PEPPER & BLACK OLIVE LAHMACUNS

SERVES 6–8 AS PART OF A MEZZE PLATTER

For the dough
125ml (4fl oz) warm water
2 tablespoons olive oil
½ teaspoon caster sugar
7g (¼oz) fast-action dried yeast
250g (8oz) strong white bread flour,
 plus extra for dusting
1 teaspoon salt

For the topping
2 tablespoons olive oil
3 red peppers
1 garlic clove, chopped
2 tablespoons tomato purée
1 teaspoon tamarind paste
1 teaspoon soft brown sugar
150g (5oz) pitted kalamata olives,
 roughly chopped
3 tablespoons chopped flat leaf parsley
1 tablespoon chopped mint leaves

Preheat the oven to 220°C/fan 200°C/Gas Mark 7. Oil a baking tray.

For the dough, put the warm water, olive oil and sugar in a bowl and stir together until the sugar is dissolved. Add the yeast and leave to activate (about 5–10 minutes).

In a separate bowl, measure out the flour and salt. Create a well in the centre and pour in the yeast liquid. Incorporate it into the flour with a spoon until a sticky dough is formed. Turn out onto a floured surface and knead until smooth and elastic. Leave in a warm place for about 30 minutes, or until doubled in size.

Meanwhile, prepare the topping. Pour the olive oil on to the base of a roasting tin, add the peppers and mix together thoroughly. Roast the peppers for 10–15 minutes until they start to collapse, then remove them from the oven, tip them into a bowl and cover with clingfilm. When cool enough to handle, peel off the skins and discard the seeds. Roughly chop the pepper flesh and mix together with the other topping ingredients in a bowl.

Increase the oven heat to 240°C/fan 220°C/Gas Mark 9. Divide the dough into egg-sized balls, then roll each out on a lightly floured work surface into a very thin circle, around 5mm (¼ inch) thick. Place the bases on the prepared baking tray and spread over the topping evenly, all the way to the edges. Bake for 10–15 minutes until lightly golden. Serve immediately.

Introduced to us by one of our chefs Nasaralla Soliman, this recipe is an adaptation of a typical dish from his home country of Egypt. It's great served as a cold starter with some rocket salad or as a side dish in a mezze platter like this.

STUFFED BABY AUBERGINES

SERVES 8–10 AS PART OF A MEZZE PLATTER

24 baby aubergines
light olive oil
1 red pepper, cored, deseeded and
  finely diced
1 yellow pepper, cored, deseeded and
  finely diced
½ red chilli, trimmed, deseeded and
  finely diced
handful of coriander leaves, finely
  chopped
handful of flat leaf parsley leaves,
  finely chopped
2 spring onions, trimmed and finely
  chopped
1 garlic clove, very finely chopped
grated rind of ½ lemon and juice of
  1 lemon
salt and pepper

Preheat the oven to 200°C/fan 180°C/Gas Mark 6.

Using a sharp knife, make an incision about 1cm (¹/₂ inch) deep into each aubergine lengthways. Place the aubergines on a baking tray, drizzle over a little olive oil, and roast for 15–20 minutes, until the aubergines are soft but still retain their shape. Leave to cool.

Put all the remaining ingredients in a mixing bowl, mix together well and season with salt and pepper to taste. Spoon the stuffing into the holes in each aubergine. Cover with clingfilm and leave to chill in the refrigerator until needed. Serve cold.

Our version of this traditional Greek home-style recipe has been adapted slightly over the years to include caramelized onions. We have also tried making it with a variety of feta cheeses, finding it to be particularly good when made with a soft, almost creamy feta. Filo can be tricky to use as it tears and dries out quickly – just remember to keep any unused sheets covered with clingfilm or baking paper with a damp tea towel over the top. If you tear a piece, simply patch it up with another, gluing them together with a brush of melted butter. This will rarely, if ever, show in the final product.

SPANAKOPITA

MAKES 24 INDIVIDUAL SPANAKOPITA

1 x 400g (13oz) packet filo pastry, thawed if frozen
125g (4fl oz) butter, melted
2 teaspoons sesame seeds

For the filling
olive oil
2 large onions, finely sliced
1 teaspoon caster sugar
1 teaspoon salt
500g (1lb) spinach, rinsed and drained
2 garlic cloves, very finely chopped
120g (4oz) feta cheese, crumbled
1 bunch of dill leaves, chopped
25g (1oz) pine nuts, lightly toasted
¼ teaspoon grated nutmeg
pinch of black pepper

Preheat the oven to 190°C/fan 170°C/Gas Mark 5. Line a baking tray with baking parchment. For the filling, heat a splash of olive oil in a pan, add the onions, sugar and salt and cook over a medium heat, stirring occasionally, for 15 minutes, until the onions are caramelized and golden brown. Remove from the heat and set aside.

Cook the spinach leaves in a pan of boiling water for 1 minute until tender. Strain and leave to cool, then squeeze out any excess liquid with your hands. Roughly chop the spinach and place in a mixing bowl with the caramelized onion and the rest of the filling ingredients. Mix together well.

Cut the filo pastry sheets lengthways into 4 even strips about 7cm (3 inches) wide. Brush an individual strip with melted butter, place a small spoonful of the mix towards one end of the strip and fold the corner of the pastry over it to form a triangle. Continue to fold the pastry strip over itself at right angles, making sure you brush it with more melted butter once more before you make the last fold to ensure it sticks together well. Place the triangle seam-side down on to the prepared baking tray. Repeat with the remaining strips.

Brush the tops of the prepared spanakopita with the remaining melted butter and sprinkle over the sesame seeds. Bake in the oven for 30–40 minutes, until golden brown. Serve warm.

We find using dried broad beans makes all the difference as they give the falafel a lighter texture. Just remember to start soaking them the day before you want to make them. Dried chickpeas can also be used, giving a heavier texture. Serve these Falafel with Tahini Dressing (see page 100) and Ruby Jewelled Tabbouleh (see page 96) as a starter, or wrap them up in pitta bread with shredded lettuce, tomato, tahini and Harissa (see page 228) as a filling lunch.

FALAFEL

**MAKES APPROXIMATELY
20 FALAFEL**

300g (10oz) dried broad beans
1 small potato, peeled
½ onion, diced
1 garlic clove, very finely chopped
2 teaspoons ground coriander
1 teaspoon ground cumin
pinch of cayenne pepper
2 tablespoons plain or wheat-free flour,
  plus extra for dusting
2 tablespoons lemon juice
handful of coriander leaves
1 litre (1¾ pints) sunflower oil,
  for deep-frying
salt and pepper

Put the broad beans in a bowl, cover with plenty of water and leave to soak for at least 24 hours.

The next day, put the whole peeled potato in a saucepan of boiling salted water and cook for 10–15 minutes until tender and cooked through. Drain, mash and set aside.

Drain the soaked broad beans and tip them into a food processor. Blend them together to your preferred consistency, either leaving the mixture slightly coarse (this will give the falafels more bite) or blending it further until it resembles fine breadcrumbs.

Add the onion, garlic, spices, flour, lemon juice and coriander leaves to the broad beans, season with salt and pepper and blend together to combine. Tip the mixture into a bowl, add the potato and mix together well using your hands. Roll the falafel mixture into bite-sized pieces on a lightly floured work surface.

Fill a large saucepan or deep-fryer with the sunflower oil and heat to 180°C (350°F), or until a cube of bread thrown into the oil browns in 30 seconds. Deep-fry the falafel in batches in the hot oil for about 3–4 minutes, or until golden brown all over. Remove with a slotted spoon and drain on kitchen paper. Serve.

It's best to make these marinated beauties in advance to allow the flavours plenty of time to develop. They will keep really well in the refrigerator for a week or so.

MARINATED MUSHROOMS

MAKES 1 X 600ML (1 PINT) JAR

250g (8oz) chestnut mushrooms
250g (8oz) button mushrooms
2 bay leaves
1 small cinnamon stick
4 thyme sprigs
30g (1oz) golden granulated sugar
250ml (8fl oz) balsamic vinegar
500ml (17fl oz) water

To serve
1 tablespoon extra virgin olive oil
1 tablespoon chopped parsley leaves

Wash the mushrooms thoroughly, trimming the ends if necessary to make sure they are free from dirt.

Put the cleaned mushrooms in a small saucepan along with the remaining ingredients. Bring to a simmer, cover with a plate small enough to fit inside the pan (this will weigh down on the mushrooms and help them absorb more of the juices) and leave to cook for 15–20 minutes.

Remove from the heat and set aside to cool, then tip into a suitable airtight container and refrigerate for at least 12 hours. Drizzle over a little olive oil and scatter over some chopped parsley before serving.

If you've only ever had cold stuffed vine leaves from the supermarket or, heaven forbid, the mushy canned variety, then you need to give these a go because they are totally delicious. Although they are best served warm you can make them in advance, refrigerate, then let them come up to room temperature – just don't serve them fridge cold, as the rice will be hard. You can use a ceramic baking dish for this recipe, though as it is helpful to be able to see the water level through the dish, a Pyrex dish is recommended.

SUNBLUSHED TOMATO
& PINE NUT STUFFED VINE LEAVES

SERVES 8–10 AS PART OF A MEZZE PLATTER

30–35 vine leaves in brine
2 tablespoons olive oil
1 large white onion, finely diced
4 garlic cloves, finely chopped
¼ teaspoon ground cumin
250g (8oz) sunblushed tomatoes in oil, drained and chopped, oil reserved
300g (10oz) long-grain white rice, rinsed and drained
2 tablespoons chopped flat leaf parsley leaves
2 tablespoons chopped dill leaves
75g (3oz) pine nuts, lightly toasted and roughly chopped
grated rind of ½ lemon

Preheat the oven to 190°C/fan 170°C/Gas Mark 5. Soak the vine leaves in boiling water and drain them according to the packet instructions.

Heat the oil in a pan, add the onion, garlic and cumin and cook over a gentle heat, stirring, for 5–8 minutes, until the onions are soft and translucent. Add the sunblushed tomatoes and cook for another minute or so, then remove from the heat and stir in the rice, herbs, nuts and grated lemon rind.

Spread out the vine leaves, trimming off the stalk at the base of each with a pair of scissors. Spoon a tablespoon or so of the filling into the centre of each, fold the ends over and roll the leaves up, pressing the mixture into a sausage shape as you go. Arrange the rolls seam-side down in a 22 x 33-cm (9 x 13-inch) ovenproof dish, packing them together as tightly as possible to stop them moving around while cooking. (The dish must be tightly packed or the vine leaves will fall apart – if you have any empty room left in the dish then pack it out with scrunched up baking parchment.)

Pour over enough water to cover the vine leaves by about 3mm (¹/8 inch) and drizzle over the oil from the sunblushed tomatoes. Cover with baking parchment and weigh down with a smaller ovenproof dish or a couple of plates to stop the vine leaves floating about. Bake for 1 hour, adding extra water halfway through cooking if the vine leaves are starting to dry out. Serve warm.

If you're in a rush, you can use ready-cooked beetroot here but the flavour, colour and texture is much better if you cook them yourself.

BEETROOT & DILL DIP

SERVES 4–6

400g (13oz) beetroot
200g (7oz) Greek yogurt
handful of dill leaves, chopped
grated rind and juice of ½ lemon
salt and white pepper

Put the beetroot in a large saucepan, cover with water and bring to the boil. Reduce to a simmer and cook for 20–30 minutes over a medium heat until tender enough for a knife to pierce the centre of each beetroot easily. Drain and leave to cool.

Grate the cooked beetroot into a mixing bowl, add the yogurt, dill leaves and grated lemon rind and juice. Stir together well. Season to taste with salt and white pepper and serve.

The amount of lemon juice and tahini used when making hummus is quite personal, so if you feel the need to adjust the amounts to suit your taste please do so. The key factor to getting a superior hummus is finding first-rate ingredients, so it's definitely worth hunting out good-quality chickpeas to give the hummus a smooth texture and great taste.

HUMMUS

SERVES 6–8

2 x 400g (13oz) cans chickpeas
juice of 1 small lemon
3 tablespoons light tahini paste
¼ teaspoon ground cumin
1 small garlic clove, very finely chopped
300ml (½ pint) light olive oil
salt and white pepper

Tip the chickpeas into a food processor and briefly pulse, then add the remainder of the ingredients and season with salt and white pepper. Blend until smooth, taste and adjust the seasoning if necessary. Serve with warm flatbread or as part of a mezze platter.

If you prefer not to use chickpeas, use white beans such as **butter beans** or **haricot beans** in this recipe.

Adapt your hummus by spicing it up with some **chilli** and **coriander** or sweetening it with some **roast pepper**.

To give your hummus an impressive finishing touch, top it with a few reserved chickpeas mixed with a drizzle of olive oil, some chilli flakes and toasted cumin seeds.

Using a stand mixer to make this dip gives it a light, moussy texture that cannot be achieved with a stick blender, as the air is needed to give it a creamier finish. If you don't have a stand mixer, whisk all the ingredients together in a bowl with an electric or hand whisk for a similar effect.

CHILLI & FETA DIP

SERVES 4

350g (11½oz) feta cheese
pinch of dried chilli flakes
pinch of cayenne pepper
pinch of sweet paprika
1 small garlic clove, very finely chopped
1 tablespoon chopped flat leaf parsley
100ml (3½fl oz) olive oil
warmed flatbreads, to serve

Put all the ingredients in the bowl of a stand mixer. Using the beater attachment, mix together for 5 minutes on a slow speed to combine, then mix together for another 20–25 minutes until the dip is light and mousse-like. Serve with warmed flatbreads.

This also makes a delicious spread for sandwiches and wraps.

Give more kick to this dip by adding extra chilli or cayenne pepper.

SALADS

A delicious, summery salad full of fresh green flavours and contrasting textures. If you eat dairy and fancy having this as a main course, try topping it with a little grilled or fried haloumi cheese. For a vegan option, this makes a wonderful accompaniment to homemade Falafel (see page 72).

WILD RICE SALAD WITH PEAS, PEA SHOOTS & GREEN HARISSA

SERVES 6–8 AS A STARTER

300g (10oz) wild rice
6 spring onions, trimmed
1 cucumber
1 bunch of flat leaf parsley leaves
1 bunch of coriander leaves
1 bunch of mint leaves
2 green chillies, trimmed
150g (5oz) frozen baby garden peas,
  defrosted
100ml (3½fl oz) Green Harissa
  (*see* page 229)
grated rind and juice of 1 lemon
salt
50g (2oz) pea shoots, to garnish

Bring a saucepan of salted water to a boil. Add the rice, lower the heat to a simmer and cook for 20–30 minutes until the rice is tender. Drain the rice and leave to cool.

While the rice is cooling, thinly slice the spring onions and roughly chop the cucumber and herbs. Finely chop the chillies and tip into a bowl with the chopped herbs, cucumber, spring onion slices, peas and cooled rice. Toss together with the Green Harissa, grated lemon rind and lemon juice, then garnish with the pea shoots and serve.

If you eat dairy then this salad is great with **feta** or **grilled haloumi**.

If you would like to save time, dress this salad with **lemon juice** and **olive oil** rather than green harissa.

To make in advance, layer all the ingredients except the lemon juice and rind on top of the rice in the serving bowl then just toss before serving, adding the lemon juice and rind at this stage. This will ensure that the colours stay vibrant.

Yes, yes, we know, lentil salad may seem a bit clichéd, but this is so tangy and moreish we couldn't possibly think of leaving it out. It's great either warm or cold and, if you don't mind a bit of dairy, works brilliantly with goats' cheese too. You can substitute anything you like for the vegetables here – just try to stick to veggies that will hold their shape when mixed together with the lentils.

PUY LENTIL SALAD
WITH ROASTED VEGETABLES

SERVES 6–8 AS A STARTER

200g (7oz) Puy lentils
1 red onion, very finely diced
80ml (3fl oz) olive oil
80ml (3fl oz) balsamic vinegar
1 red chilli, trimmed and chopped
3 garlic cloves, chopped
2 tablespoons dark brown sugar
3 tablespoons tomato purée
1 tablespoon fennel seeds, toasted and
  lightly crushed
1 bunch of flat leaf parsley leaves
75g (3oz) baby spinach leaves, red chard
  leaves or bull's blood leaves
salt

For the roasted vegetables
olive oil
300g (10oz) pumpkin or butternut
  squash, peeled and cut into 2-cm-
  (¾-inch-) thick wedges
½ fennel bulb, trimmed and cut into
  1-cm- (½-inch-) thick wedges
150g (5oz) cherry tomatoes
1 courgette, cut into 1-cm- (½-inch-)
  thick wedges
2 red or yellow peppers, cored,
  deseeded and cut into 1-cm- (½-inch-)
  thick wedges

Preheat the oven to 200°C/fan 180°C/Gas Mark 6.

Bring a saucepan of salted water to a boil and add the lentils. Lower the heat and simmer for 15–20 minutes until tender. Drain and put in a large salad bowl.

Put the onion, olive oil, balsamic vinegar, chilli, garlic, sugar, tomato purée and crushed fennel seeds in a small saucepan. Bring to a simmer and cook gently, stirring frequently, for 4–5 minutes until the sugar has dissolved. Spoon the warm dressing over the lentils and leave to cool.

For the roasted vegetables, drizzle a little oil on to the base of a roasting tin. Add the pumpkin or squash pieces, season with salt and mix together thoroughly. Roast for 10 minutes. Toss the fennel and whole tomatoes in a little oil, add to the tin and roast for another 10 minutes. Finally, toss the courgettes and peppers in a little oil, add to the tin and roast for a further 10 minutes. By now the vegetables should all be tender and cooked through. Set aside to cool slightly.

Roughly chop the parsley and add to the salad bowl along with the salad leaves and roasted vegetables. Mix everything together well and serve.

Quinoa is an ancient, Incan grain-like crop grown for its seeds, which are boiled or steamed until they have something like the texture of couscous. Unlike couscous, though, quinoa is both amazingly nutritious – full of protein, iron and magnesium, among other things – and gluten-free. Here it is combined with kidney beans and peppers and covered in our chipotle lime dressing to create a zingy, chunky salad full of flavour and texture.

PERUVIAN QUINOA SALAD WITH KIDNEY BEANS, PEPPERS & CHIPOTLE LIME DRESSING

SERVES 6–8 AS A STARTER

300g (10oz) white, red or black
  quinoa grains
1 sweet potato, peeled and cut into
  3-cm (1-inch) cubes
olive oil
1 large red pepper, cored, deseeded and
  cut into 3-cm (1-inch) chunks
1 large yellow pepper, cored, deseeded
  and cut into 3-cm (1-inch) chunks
grated rind and juice of 1 lime
1 bunch of coriander leaves, roughly
  chopped
3 red chillies, trimmed and finely
  chopped
2 red onions, finely diced
400g (13oz) can kidney beans, drained
  and rinsed
75g (3oz) bull's blood leaves, red chard
  or baby spinach leaves
100ml (3½fl oz) Chipotle Lime Dressing
  (*see* page 240)
salt and pepper

Preheat the oven to 190°C/fan 170°C/Gas Mark 5. Line a baking tray with baking parchment.

Cook the quinoa in boiling water according to the packet instructions, then drain well and leave to cool. Season with salt and pepper.

Toss the sweet potato pieces in a little oil, arrange on the prepared baking tray and roast in the oven for 15–20 minutes or so, until just starting to soften. Toss the peppers in a little oil, add to the baking tray with the sweet potatoes and roast for a further 10 minutes or so, until tender. Leave to cool on the tray, then tip into a large salad bowl with the quinoa and all the remaining ingredients. Mix everything together well. Serve.

This salad has been a staple on our menu for many, many years. It is 100 per cent organic in the restaurant as we use only organic fruit and veg to prepare it; if you're making it up at home then this choice is entirely up to you. For those of you who own a mandolin, use it here to cut your fennel into perfect paper-thin slices. Just be careful of your fingers!

DETOX SALAD

SERVES 6–8 AS A STARTER

6 carrots, peeled and grated
3 medium beetroot, peeled and grated
1 small fennel bulb, very finely sliced
50g (2oz) mixed bean sprouts
100g (3½oz) sultanas
25g (1oz) sunflower seeds, toasted
25g (1oz) pumpkin seeds, toasted
50ml (2fl oz) extra virgin olive oil
handful of coriander leaves,
 to garnish

For the dressing
1-cm (½-inch) piece of fresh root ginger
juice of 2 large oranges
60ml (2½fl oz) non-pasteurized
 apple juice
40ml (1½fl oz) lime juice

To make the dressing, peel and finely dice the ginger. Using the flat side of your knife, press down on the ginger pieces to release any excess juice. (Alternatively, if you have a juicing machine, peel and juice the ginger.) Put the diced or juiced ginger into a small jar along with the remainder of the dressing ingredients, pop the lid on and shake well.

Assemble all the salad ingredients in a large mixing bowl and toss together well. Drizzle over the dressing and serve, garnished with coriander leaves.

This salad is a riot of fantastic, jewel-like colours and bright, fresh flavours. It's becoming easier to find golden and striped varieties of beetroot at greengrocers and even in supermarkets, but if you are having trouble sourcing them don't worry too much; normal red beetroot won't make any difference in terms of flavour (though they won't look quite so pretty). Likewise if blood oranges are out of season simply use regular oranges in their place.

WARM RUBY & GOLDEN BEETROOT SALAD
WITH ROAST HAZELNUTS, BLOOD ORANGES & LABNEH

SERVES 6–8 AS A STARTER

1.5kg (3lb) mixed beetroot (such as Candy, Bull's Blood and Golden)
5 tablespoons olive oil
5 tablespoons date syrup
125g (4oz) skinned hazelnuts
5 blood oranges
100g (3½oz) baby spinach leaves
400g (13oz) Homemade Labneh Cheese (*see* page 43)
sea salt flakes

Preheat the oven to 190°C/fan 170°C/Gas Mark 5. Line 2 baking trays with baking parchment.

Bring a large saucepan of water to the boil, add the beetroot and boil until they are beginning to soften (about 20–30 minutes for medium beetroot and 40 minutes for large – you'll know they are ready when a knife stuck into them comes out pretty easily). Drain and leave to cool, then peel, cut in half and slice into 1-cm- (½-inch-) thick half moons.

Arrange the beetroot slices on one of the baking trays, drizzle with the olive oil and date syrup and sprinkle with sea salt flakes. Roast for 15 minutes, until golden brown at the edges.

Meanwhile, spread the hazelnuts out on the other baking tray and roast for 5 minutes, until lightly golden. Remove from the oven and leave to cool slightly.

Cut the skins and pith off the oranges and slice the orange flesh horizontally into thin strips. Put in a salad bowl and toss together with the beetroot, hazelnuts and spinach leaves. Spoon the Homemade Labneh Cheese over the salad and serve.

It's great to see that heirloom potatoes are becoming more widely available – there are some wonderful old varieties out there, many of which both look and taste fantastic. This salad celebrates them, and we like to make it with a mix of violet, ruby and new potatoes. If you're struggling to find heritage potatoes then just use new potatoes instead.

HEIRLOOM POTATO & ROAST ASPARAGUS
SALAD WITH TRUFFLE MAYONNAISE

SERVES 6–8 AS A STARTER

500g (1lb) mixed heirloom potatoes
  (such as Salad Blue, Arran Victory or
  Pink Fir Apples)
500g (1lb) new potatoes
16 asparagus spears
olive oil
6 spring onions, trimmed and sliced
1 bunch of chives, finely chopped, plus
  a few extra to garnish
75g (3oz) watercress, plus a few extra
  leaves to garnish
grated rind of ½ lemon
100ml (3½fl oz) Truffle Mayonnaise
  (*see* page 235)
sea salt flakes

Preheat the oven to 200°C/fan 180°C/Gas Mark 6. Line a baking tray with baking parchment.

Bring a saucepan of salted water to a boil, add the potatoes and cook for 20–30 minutes, depending on size, until tender. Drain and cut into bite-sized pieces.

To prepare the asparagus, snap off the woody base of the stalks. Lay the spears on the prepared baking tray, sprinkle with sea salt flakes and drizzle with a little olive oil. Roast for 5–10 minutes until tender but still firm. Leave to cool, then slice into thirds.

Put the potatoes and asparagus in a large salad bowl with the spring onions, chives, watercress and grated lemon rind. Add the Truffle Mayonnaise and toss well to coat. Scatter over a few extra watercress leaves and chives to finish. Serve.

While pasta salad might seem a little old-fashioned, this simple, sophisticated dish is full of beautiful flavours and colours. It's worth hunting down purple basil leaves – also sometimes confusingly called red basil – to use here, as they will give the oil and salad a lovely dark pink colour. For an extra-mushroomy hit, add a few drops of truffle oil to taste when mixing your ingredients together before serving.

OYSTER MUSHROOM FUSILLI SALAD
WITH PURPLE BROCCOLI, BASIL & PINE NUTS

SERVES 6–8 AS A STARTER

300g (10oz) fusilli
300g (10oz) purple sprouting broccoli
2 tablespoons olive oil
3 garlic cloves, chopped
250g (8oz) oyster mushrooms, trimmed
  and roughly shredded
100ml (3½fl oz) Purple Basil Oil
  (*see* page 238)
25g (1oz) toasted pine nuts
grated rind of ½ lemon
10 purple basil leaves
salt

Add the pasta to a large saucepan of boiling salted water and cook according to the packet instructions until al dente. Drain and set aside. In another saucepan, blanch the broccoli for 2–3 minutes in boiling salted water until tender. Set aside.

Heat the olive oil in a wok or frying pan over a medium–high heat, add the garlic and cook, stirring, for 1 minute. Add the oyster mushrooms and cook for 2–3 minutes, until they are beginning to brown. Remove from the heat. If the mushrooms have released a lot of liquid while cooking, drain in a colander.

Chop the broccoli into 4-cm (½-inch) pieces, tip into a large salad bowl and toss together with the Purple Basil Oil, mushrooms, pasta, pine nuts and grated lemon rind. Tear the basil leaves into strips, toss them through the salad and serve.

This ruby tabbouleh is a beautiful twist on the traditional bulgar wheat salad, its vibrant colours and fresh, herby flavours providing the perfect antidote to a dull autumn or winter's day. Should you feel like giving the salad a bit more substance, the grassy herbs and sweet fruit go very well with the sharp tang of feta cheese.

RUBY JEWELLED TABBOULEH

SERVES 6–8 AS A STARTER

250g (8oz) bulgar wheat
1 large bunch of flat leaf parsley,
  leaves picked
1 large bunch of mint, leaves picked
grated rind and juice of 2 oranges
grated rind and juice of 1 lemon
2 red chillies, trimmed and finely
  chopped
3 red onions, finely chopped
3 large beef tomatoes or 8 vine
  tomatoes, deseeded and finely diced
50ml (2fl oz) olive oil
¼ teaspoon sumac
pinch of ground cinnamon
pinch of ground cumin
600g (1¼lb) red seedless grapes,
  cut in half
100g (3½oz) pomegranate seeds
100g (3½oz) pistachios, toasted and
  lightly crushed
salt

Rinse the bulgar wheat thoroughly and drain in a fine sieve.

Bring a large saucepan of salted water to the boil. Add the bulgar wheat, reduce the heat to a simmer and cook for 10–15 minutes, until the bulgar wheat is tender but still retains a bite. Take off the heat and leave the grains to steam in the pan for 2–3 minutes, then tip into a fine sieve, rinse with cold water and leave to drain.

Meanwhile, roughly chop the parsley and mint leaves, and put in a salad bowl with the remaining ingredients. Add the drained bulgar wheat and toss everything together well to mix. Serve.

A lot of people don't like okra but that's probably because they've either only had the stringy old stuff, or it's been overcooked. When buying okra, be picky and only select the smaller green fingers. To prepare, just remove the stem rather than cutting off the entire top to stop the okra from releasing liquid while frying. Finally, make sure you wash your okra just before you use it and no earlier – if it sits around in water it will quickly discolour and become gluey.

SPICED OKRA WITH CHERRY TOMATOES, BABY SPINACH & MINT

SERVES 6–8 AS A STARTER

light oil (such as rapeseed, groundnut or sunflower)
300g (10oz) okra, stems removed
1 teaspoon medium Madras curry powder
300g (10oz) mixed red and yellow cherry tomatoes, halved
½ cucumber, peeled, deseeded and cut into 1-cm (½-inch) slices
4 spring onions, trimmed and thinly sliced
handful of mint leaves
2 red chillies, trimmed and thinly sliced
50g (2oz) baby spinach leaves or baby chard leaves
2–3 tablespoons Lemon Mint Dressing (*see* page 242)
sea salt flakes

Heat a drizzle of light oil in a wok or large frying pan over a medium heat. Wash the okra, drain briefly and put in the hot pan still slightly wet. Cook, stirring, for 5 minutes, until the okra has puffed up and is beginning to collapse. Add the curry powder and cook for another 30 seconds or so. Remove from the heat.

Add a large pinch of sea salt flakes to the okra and let cool slightly, then tip it into a large salad bowl and toss together with the other ingredients. Serve.

This is a nice simple salad full of chunky vegetables and Middle Eastern flavours. The black skins of the aubergine are a wonderful contrast to the red of the tomatoes and the green of the cucumbers. We like to use baby plum tomatoes here for their richer, sweeter flavour but, if you can get hold of them, good ripe cherry tomatoes will work well too.

ROAST AUBERGINE, CUCUMBER & BABY PLUM TOMATO SALAD WITH TAHINI DRESSING

SERVES 6–8 AS A STARTER

2 large aubergines
½ teaspoon smoked paprika
½ teaspoon ground cumin
2–3 tablespoons olive oil
1 bunch of flat leaf parsley leaves,
  roughly chopped
handful of mint leaves, roughly
  chopped
2 bunches of spring onions, trimmed
  and sliced
1 large cucumber, deseeded and cut
  into 2.5-cm (1-inch) cubes
750g (1½lb) baby plum tomatoes,
  cut in half
75g (3oz) baby spinach leaves
grated rind of ½ lemon
salt and pepper
Tahini Dressing (*see* page 243),
  to serve

Cut the aubergines into 2.5-cm (1-inch) cubes, sprinkle with salt and leave to stand in a colander set over a bowl for 20 minutes (this will remove any bitter juices and stop the aubergine from absorbing as much oil during cooking).

Preheat the oven to 200°C/fan 180°C/Gas Mark 5. Line two baking trays with baking parchment.

Rinse the aubergines to remove the salt and toss them into a bowl with the paprika, cumin and olive oil. Mix together well. Spoon out evenly on to the prepared baking trays and roast for 15–20 minutes, until the aubergines are soft but not mushy. Set aside to cool.

Once cool, tip the aubergines into a large bowl and mix together with the remaining salad ingredients. Season to taste with salt and pepper. Drizzle the dressing over the salad and serve.

This is an absolute classic and still one of our most popular salads. The homemade croutons toasted in our herb oil elevate it to special status. We like to use day-old sourdough bread to make our croutons, but it's worth playing around and using whatever leftover loaf you have to hand (you can even use gluten-free bread if you like); just bear in mind that an airy bread with a lot of texture will give the best results.

CAESAR SALAD WITH AVOCADO & FRENCH BEANS

SERVES 6–8 AS A STARTER

4 eggs
200g (7oz) French beans, trimmed
2 romaine or 4 baby gem lettuces, trimmed
2 ripe avocados, peeled and sliced
100g (3½oz) vegetarian Parmesan-style hard cheese, shaved
200ml (7fl oz) Vegetarian Caesar Dressing (*see* page 240)
salt

For the croutons
200g (7oz) sourdough bread
100ml (3½fl oz) Herb Oil (*see* page 238)
large pinch of sea salt flakes

Preheat the oven to 180°C/fan 160°C/Gas Mark 4.

For the croutons, cut the bread into 2.5-cm (1-inch) cubes and mix together with the Herb Oil and sea salt flakes in a bowl. Spread on to a baking tray and toast in the oven for 15 minutes, turning about halfway through, until lightly golden on all sides.

Meanwhile, bring a saucepan of lightly salted water to the boil, add the eggs and cook for 4–5 minutes (the yolks should be set but still quite soft). Take off the heat and let sit for a minute, then rinse in cold running water and shell under the tap while still warm.

Bring another saucepan of lightly salted water to the boil, add the beans and blanch for 2–3 minutes until tender. Rinse in cold running water and set aside.

Cut the eggs into quarters lengthways and the lettuces into thick wedges. Toss the lettuce wedges in a large bowl with the avocado, beans, three-quarters of the shaved cheese and the dressing. Divide the croutons and egg pieces evenly between serving plates and scatter over the rest of the cheese. Serve.

Like labneh (see page 43), ricotta is super-easy to make at home and doesn't require any fancy equipment except a bit of muslin cloth. In fact, when we were testing out this recipe one quiet Sunday we found we didn't have any muslin, so improvised and washed one of our cotton tote bags and used that instead! This recipe makes more ricotta than you will need, but don't worry as you'll find lots of uses for it – it's fantastic stirred through fresh pasta with a few spring vegetables, can be added to tart or quiche fillings to give them an extra creamy, rich texture and makes a delicious stuffing for fried courgette flowers. Leftover ricotta will keep for up to 4 days in the refrigerator in a suitable container.

PRIMAVERA SALAD WITH HOMEMADE LEMON RICOTTA

SERVES 6–8 AS A STARTER

80g (3oz) broad beans, defrosted
  if frozen
150g (5oz) sugar snap peas, trimmed
  and de-strung
120g (4oz) baby garden peas, defrosted
  if frozen
12 asparagus spears
olive oil
75ml (3fl oz) Lemon Mint Dressing
  (*see* page 242)
40g (1½oz) pea shoots
sea salt flakes

For the Homemade Lemon Ricotta
2 litres (3½ pints) full-fat milk
grated rind and juice of 1 large lemon
1 teaspoon salt

To make the ricotta, put the milk, grated lemon rind and salt in a large saucepan and bring just to the point of boiling. Add the lemon juice and remove from the heat, stirring gently, until curds start to form. Cover a sieve with muslin cloth and set over a bowl. Pour the curds and whey over the cloth, then tie the opposite ends of the muslin together before tying the ends around a wooden spoon. Suspend the cloth in the air by hanging it across a sink or over a large plastic tub and leave to drain for 15–30 minutes (the longer it drains, the drier the ricotta becomes). Remove from the muslin and store in an airtight container in the refrigerator until needed.

Preheat the oven to 200°C/fan 180°C/Gas Mark 6. Line a baking tray with baking parchment. Bring a saucepan of salted water to the boil, add the beans and cook for 2–3 minutes until tender. Drain and refresh under cold water. Remove the skins and set the beans aside. Steam the sugar snap and baby garden peas for 2–3 minutes until tender.

Snap off the woody base of the asparagus stalks. Lay the spears on the baking tray, sprinkle with sea salt flakes and drizzle with olive oil. Roast for 5–10 minutes until tender but still firm. Leave to cool, then cut each spear in half. Tip into a salad bowl with the dressing, pea shoots and other vegetables and mix together, then spoon on to a serving plate. Crumble over 100g (3½oz) of the ricotta. Serve.

MAINS

A great laksa is tricky to find, and a vegetarian version even more so, as a big part of a laksa's distinct flavour comes from the shrimp paste and fish sauce that are traditionally used. We've tried many ways to substitute these flavours, adding various fermented soy bean sauces and pastes, but have come to prefer this simpler version in which the Thai hot mint and lime leaf star. The tofu puffs act like a sponge, soaking up the flavours. They can be bought in Asian supermarkets.

PEA, CARROT, PEPPER & TOFU LAKSA

SERVES 6

vegetable oil
3 x 400ml (14fl oz) cans coconut milk
800ml (1¼ pints) vegetable stock
80g (3oz) palm sugar
250g (8oz) rice noodles
2 carrots, thinly sliced
2 red peppers, cored, deseeded and diced
200g (7oz) sugar snap peas
200g (7oz) peas, defrosted if frozen
300g (10oz) tofu puffs

For the spice paste
6 lemon grass stalks
5-cm (2-inch) piece of fresh root galangal or ginger, peeled and finely chopped
4 red chillies, trimmed, deseeded and finely chopped
6 garlic cloves, finely chopped
15g (½oz) fresh turmeric, peeled or 2 teaspoons ground turmeric
15 lime leaves, middle stem removed
handful of Thai hot mint leaves
150g (5oz) red Asian shallots or regular shallots, finely chopped
3–4 tablespoons vegetable oil

To serve
3 limes, cut into halves
50g (2oz) crispy shallots
300g (10oz) bean sprouts
handful of coriander leaves, chopped

For the spice paste, remove the outer leaf of each lemon grass stalk, cut out the tough middle cores and finely slice the remainder. Tip into a food processor with the chopped galangal and blend together for 5 minutes, then add the chilli, garlic, turmeric, lime leaves, mint and shallots and continue to blend, adding the vegetable oil, to form a smooth paste.

Heat a splash of vegetable oil in a saucepan over a low heat, add the paste and cook for 15 minutes until it is toasted and lightly fragrant. Pour over the coconut milk and vegetable stock, stir in the palm sugar and bring to a simmer. Cook over a medium–low heat for 20 minutes until reduced to a fragrant, creamy broth.

Meanwhile, cook or soak the rice noodles in boiling water according to the packet instructions, then drain well and set aside. Blanch the vegetables in a saucepan of boiling water for no more than 1 minute, until just tender but still nice and crunchy. Drain.

Divide the noodles and tofu puffs between deep bowls, pour over the broth and top each with a good handful of the blanched vegetables. Garnish with lime wedges, crispy shallots, bean sprouts and chopped coriander leaves. Serve.

*Risotto cakes are a great way to use up leftover risotto
from a previous dinner, though they taste so good we make
them from scratch like this. If you did want to make up
a simple risotto, just double up and follow the basic rice
cooking method here, adding a little roasted pumpkin or
squash. Enjoy it for dinner as a risotto, then use the extra
to make these cakes the next day.*

SAFFRON & PEA RISOTTO CAKES

SERVES 6

1 litre (1¾ pints) vegetable stock
light olive oil
1 onion, diced
6 garlic cloves, crushed
pinch of saffron threads
1 teaspoon fennel seeds
400g (13oz) arborio rice
100ml (3½fl oz) white wine
70g (3oz) baby garden peas, defrosted
  if frozen
250g (8oz) fresh or dried breadcrumbs

To serve
Red Pepper Sauce (*see* page 150)
wilted spinach

Bring the stock to a simmer in a saucepan. Heat a splash of oil in
a separate saucepan, add the onion and garlic and cook, stirring, for
2–3 minutes, until the onion has started to soften. Add the saffron,
fennel seeds and rice and sauté for a further 2 minutes. Pour in
the wine and let it bubble to reduce down until the pan is quite
dry. Gradually add the stock about a ladleful at a time, stirring
frequently, until the rice is cooked but still firm.

Remove the rice from the heat and transfer to a small tray or large
plate. Leave to cool for 10 minutes then refrigerate for a further
15–20 minutes until firm.

Once cool, remove the rice from the refrigerator and mix in the peas.
Shape into cakes about 10cm (4 inches) in diameter. Roll the cakes in
the breadcrumbs until evenly coated.

Heat a thin layer of oil in a wide frying pan. Add the risotto cakes
and fry for 2–3 minutes on each side until golden brown. Serve on
individual plates with a spoonful or two of Red Pepper Sauce and a
little wilted spinach.

For a vegan alternative, pair this dish with **Tomato & Basil Sauce** (*see* page 151).

To make this gluten-free, coat the risotto cakes with **gluten-free breadcrumbs**.

One of our chefs, Alex Aimassi, first developed this as a lunchtime special, though it's now one of our most popular dishes and flies out of the door whenever we make it. If using dried lasagne sheets, add a splash of water between layers of pasta when assembling this to stop it from drying out.

TENDERSTEM BROCCOLI & ASPARAGUS WHITE LASAGNE

SERVES 8–10

700g (1½lb) asparagus spears, trimmed
  and woody ends removed
500g (1lb) Tenderstem broccoli
700g (1½lb) fresh lasagne sheets
300g (10oz) vegetarian Parmesan-style
  hard cheese, grated
300g (10oz) mature Cheddar cheese,
  grated
salt

For the caramelized onion
a splash of light cooking oil (such as
  rapeseed, groundnut or sunflower)
6 white onions, finely sliced
1 tablespoon caster sugar

For the white sauce
3 litres (5¼ pints) milk
1 white onion, cut into quarters
6 garlic cloves
3 bay leaves
800g (1¾lb) Tenderstem broccoli
280g (9oz) butter
300g (10oz) plain flour
2 bunches of basil leaves, chopped

For the caramelized onion, heat the oil in a saucepan over a medium heat, add the onions and cook for 15 minutes, stirring, until they begin to colour. Add the sugar and continue to cook for 15–20 minutes, stirring occasionally, until the onions are dark golden brown and caramelized. Remove from the heat and set aside.

Meanwhile, for the white sauce, bring the milk, onion, garlic and bay leaves to a simmer in a saucepan over a medium heat. Remove from the heat and set aside for 10 minutes for the flavours to infuse. Cook the broccoli in boiling water for 3 minutes until tender. Drain and roughly chop. Melt the butter in a saucepan, add the flour and stir together to form a roux. Strain the milk into the pan and whisk together to form a smooth sauce. Add the broccoli and basil to the sauce and blend with a stick blender until the sauce is smooth.

Bring a saucepan of salted water to the boil. Cut the asparagus widthways into thirds and the broccoli widthways into halves, add to the water and blanch for 2 minutes. Drain and set aside to cool.

Preheat the oven to 190°C/fan 170°C/Gas Mark 5. To layer the lasagne, add a splash of water to the bottom of a 30 x 22-cm (12 x 9-inch) rectangular ovenproof dish, then arrange a layer of lasagne sheets on top. Spoon over half the caramelized onion, broccoli, asparagus and half the grated cheeses, then layer with a third of the white sauce. Repeat the layers of pasta, filling and sauce, finishing with a third layer of pasta and a final layer of white sauce. Bake for 40–50 minutes, until the pasta is cooked and the top is golden brown (if the lasagne is browning too much during cooking, cover it with foil).

Remove from the oven and set aside for 10–15 minutes to cool and set slightly before cutting into portions.

We partner this creamy, coconutty curry with our Garlic Rotis (see page 184) and Tomato and Coconut Sambal (see page 231). The curry powder recipe makes enough for future use. Just store the remainder in an airtight container in your spice collection. If you are short of time, 1 tablespoon of Madras curry powder can be used instead. Turmeric, Pea & Cardamom Basmati (see page 199) makes a nice alternative to plain basmati.

SRI LANKAN SWEET POTATO & CASHEW NUT CURRY

SERVES 6–8

vegetable oil
3 large sweet potatoes, peeled and cut
  into 4-cm (1½-inch) chunks
1 large onion, diced
5-cm (2-inch) piece of fresh root ginger,
  peeled and chopped
3 garlic cloves
2 green chillies, trimmed and chopped
12 fresh or frozen curry leaves
2 teaspoons ground turmeric
1 cinnamon stick
4 x 400ml (14fl oz) cans coconut cream
100g (3½oz) creamed coconut
1 tablespoon caster sugar
300g (10oz) basmati rice, washed
  thoroughly and strained
400ml (14fl oz) boiling water
salt
250g (8oz) roasted cashew nuts,
  to garnish

For the curry powder
2 tablespoons coriander seeds
1 tablespoon fennel seeds
1 tablespoon cumin seeds
2 teaspoons fenugreek seeds
2 teaspoons black mustard seeds
5g (¼oz) fresh or frozen curry leaves

To serve (optional)
Garlic Rotis (see page 184)
Tomato & Coconut Sambal (see page 231)

First make the curry powder. Preheat the oven to 80°C/fan 60°C/Gas Mark as low as possible. Roast the spices in the oven for 30–40 minutes, being careful not to burn them, until the curry leaves have dried out completely. Remove from the oven and grind to a powder using a mortar and pestle or spice/coffee grinder.

Increase the oven temperature to 200°C/fan 180°C/Gas Mark 6. Drizzle a little vegetable oil on to the base of a roasting tin. Add the sweet potato pieces, season with salt and mix together thoroughly. Roast for 15 minutes, until cooked through. Set aside.

Blend the onion, ginger, garlic and chillies together in a food processor to form a smooth paste. Heat a splash of oil in a large saucepan, add the curry leaves and fry quickly for 10–15 seconds, being careful not to burn them. Add the paste and fry for 6–8 minutes over a medium heat until toasted and fragrant. Add the turmeric and cinnamon along with 1 tablespoon of the curry powder, season with salt and fry for a further 2–3 minutes, then stir in the coconut cream, creamed coconut and sugar. Bring to a simmer and cook for 15 minutes, until the curry has thickened and reduced.

Now, cook the rice. Place the basmati in a saucepan, cover with the boiling water, bring back to the boil and simmer, covered, for 10–12 minutes, until the water has evaporated and the rice is tender.

Meanwhile, stir the cooked sweet potato into the curry and cook for a further 6–8 minutes until heated through. Spoon the curry into bowls, garnish with roasted cashew nuts and serve with the rice, and Garlic Rotis and Tomato & Coconut Sambal, if liked.

These escalopes are packed with rich flavours and benefit from being served with something fairly simple and fresh, like a chopped tomato and cucumber salad. While we have suggested pan-frying the escalopes here for the crispiest results, the more health-conscious among you might want to roast them in the oven for 10–15 minutes at 190°C/ fan 170°C/Gas Mark 5 instead. To make this recipe gluten-free, use gluten-free breadcrumbs.

FETA, CHILLI & MINT–FILLED AUBERGINE ESCALOPE

SERVES 8

2 large aubergines
5 tablespoons olive oil
100g (3½oz) plain flour
4 eggs, beaten
600g (1¼lb) fresh white breadcrumbs
salt
mixed salad, to serve

For the filling
450g (14½oz) feta cheese, crumbled
2 red chillies, trimmed and finely
  chopped
juice of 1 lemon
4 garlic cloves, finely chopped
pinch of white pepper
1 bunch of mint leaves, finely chopped

Cut the tops off the aubergines and slice each lengthways into 8 thin slices. Sprinkle the slices with salt and leave to stand in a colander set over a bowl for 20 minutes.

Preheat the oven to 180°C/fan 160°C/Gas Mark 4.

Rinse the aubergines to remove the salt and lay them on 2 baking trays. Drizzle with 1 tablespoon of the oil and roast in the oven for 10–15 minutes, turning halfway through, until tender but not falling apart. Leave to cool on the baking trays.

For the filling, mix together all the ingredients in a bowl.

Take eight of the aubergine slices and spread a thin, even layer of the filling over each of them. Press another aubergine slice on top to make a sandwich. Coat each of the aubergine escalopes with the flour, dusting off the excess, and dip first into the beaten egg and then into the breadcrumbs.

Heat the remaining oil in a large nonstick frying pan over a low heat. Add a couple of the escalopes and gently fry for 4 minutes on each side until golden brown, then set aside on kitchen paper to drain. Repeat with the remaining escalopes and serve immediately with a mixed salad.

The Scotch egg is not, as its name suggests, from Scotland: it was invented by the London department store Fortnum & Mason in 1738. Despite its popularity, the egg's reputation has deteriorated over the years due to the proliferation of poor-quality supermarket varieties – a shame as, when cooked fresh with the yolks left slightly runny, they are unbeatable.

LEEK, CHIVE & CAPER SCOTCH EGGS
WITH MUSTARD BEURRE BLANC

SERVES 8

1kg (2lb) potatoes, peeled and cut into even-sized pieces
25g (1oz) butter
2 large leeks, trimmed, cleaned and finely diced
1 tablespoon Dijon mustard
1 tablespoon wholegrain mustard
1 bunch of chives, finely chopped
40g (½oz) capers, roughly chopped
8 large eggs, plus 3 eggs, beaten
100g (3½oz) plain flour
300g (10oz) panko breadcrumbs
2 litres (3½ pints) oil, for frying
blanched asparagus, to serve
salt and pepper

For the Mustard Beurre Blanc
175ml (6fl oz) white wine
3 large shallots, finely diced
2 tablespoons double cream
250g (8oz) cold butter, cut into cubes
1 tablespoon wholegrain mustard

Cook the potatoes in a pan of boiling water for 10–15 minutes until tender. Drain and mash with a fork or using a potato ricer until smooth. Melt the butter in a pan, add the leeks and cook, stirring, for 3–4 minutes, until just tender. Leave to cool, then tip into the mash with the mustards, chives and capers. Mix together and leave to cool.

While the mash is cooling, cook the whole eggs in a saucepan of boiling water for 4 minutes. Drain and refresh in cold water, then shell. Divide the cooled mash into eight portions. Arrange the flour, beaten egg and breadcrumbs in shallow bowls. Roll the eggs in the flour. Flatten a portion of mash with your palm and fold it around the egg to form a ball. Roll the ball in the flour, then dip first into the beaten egg and then the breadcrumbs. Place on a tray and repeat with the remaining eggs, then transfer to the refrigerator to chill.

For the beurre blanc, bring the wine and shallots to the boil in a saucepan. Cook for 3–5 minutes until reduced by two-thirds. Lower the heat, pour in the cream and gradually add the butter, whisking continuously, to form a smooth sauce. If it looks as though the sauce is going to split at any point, add a little more cream. When all the butter is mixed through, remove from the heat, stir in the mustard and season with salt and pepper to taste. Set aside in a warm place.

Half-fill a large saucepan or deep-fryer with vegetable oil and heat to 180°C (350°F), or until a cube of bread thrown into the oil browns in 30 seconds. Cook the eggs in batches for 5 minutes until golden brown. Drizzle over the beurre blanc and serve with blanched asparagus.

Definitely the sort of thing Jane would call a 'winter warmer', this cosy, spicy, slightly sweet stew will keep the cold at bay on even the dullest and chilliest of days. If you're planning on entertaining then this is a great dish to make up ahead of time and simply reheat when your guests arrive, as the flavours will continue to develop long after cooking.

CINNAMON-SPICED
SQUASH & BUTTER BEAN STEW

SERVES 6–8

light oil (such as rapeseed, groundnut
 or sunflower)
1 large butternut squash, peeled,
 deseeded and cut into 2.5-cm
 (1-inch) chunks
1 onion, diced
3 garlic cloves, very finely chopped
1 red pepper, cored, deseeded and diced
1 yellow pepper, cored, deseeded
 and diced
6 thyme sprigs
1 large rosemary sprig
2 bay leaves
1 cinnamon stick
1 teaspoon ground cinnamon
1 tablespoon smoked paprika
3 x 400g (13oz) cans chopped tomatoes
100g (3½oz) pitted kalamata olives
50ml (2fl oz) maple syrup
400ml (14fl oz) water
3 x 400g (13oz) cans butter beans,
 drained and rinsed
salt and pepper

To serve
Chilli Cornbread (*see* page 178)
fresh green salad

Preheat the oven to 200°C/fan 180°C/Gas Mark 6.

Splash a little oil on to the base of a roasting tin, add the squash pieces, season with salt and mix together thoroughly. Roast for 20 minutes, until the pumpkin is soft and cooked through. Set aside.

Heat a drizzle of oil in a frying pan, add the onion, garlic and peppers and cook gently, stirring, for 5–6 minutes, until the onion has softened slightly. Add the herbs and spices, season with salt and pepper and cook for another 5 minutes. Add the tomatoes, olives, maple syrup and water, bring to a simmer and cook over a low heat for 30 minutes, stirring occasionally, until the sauce has thickened and reduced.

Stir in the roasted butternut squash and butter beans and cook for a further 1–2 minutes until the squash is heated through. Spoon into bowls and serve with Chilli Cornbread and a fresh green salad.

This classic Italian dish is just as good cold as hot, so can be made a day in advance and then served straight from the refrigerator alongside focaccia or with a simple rocket salad. While warm, it is great with our creamy Wet Polenta (see page 197). If you can't get the baby aubergines you can substitute normal aubergines, cutting them first into half and then into wedges before using so they hold together in the sauce.

BABY AUBERGINE & ROAST PEPPER CAPONATA

SERVES 6–8

olive oil
2 red peppers
2 yellow peppers
800g (1¾lb) baby aubergines
1 large white onion, finely diced
6 garlic cloves, finely chopped
handful of fresh basil leaves, chopped
4 celery sticks, trimmed, peeled
 and sliced
1 tablespoon white wine vinegar
1 tablespoon caster sugar
100g (3½oz) tomato purée
350g (11½oz) baby plum tomatoes or
 cherry tomatoes
10 pitted green olives
20 capers
1 small bunch of flat leaf parsley leaves,
 finely chopped
sea salt and pepper
Wet Polenta (*see* page 197), to serve

Preheat the oven to 240°C/fan 220°C/Gas Mark 9.

Drizzle a little olive oil on to the base of a roasting tin. Add the peppers and mix together thoroughly. Roast for 15 minutes, until the peppers have puffed up and are starting to split open. Transfer them to a bowl, cover with clingfilm and set aside to cool for 15 minutes. Once cool enough to handle, tear the peppers open, removing the cores and seeds. Peel off the skins and cut the pepper flesh into 1.5-cm- (³/₄-inch-) thick strips. Set aside.

Peel half the skin off the aubergines in stripes and cut in half lengthways. Rinse the aubergines under running water, drain and sprinkle with a little sea salt. Heat a generous glug of olive oil in a large casserole dish. Add the aubergines and sauté for 3–5 minutes, until they begin to soften. Remove from the pan and set aside.

Add the onion and garlic to the pan and sauté for 5 minutes, until the onion begins to soften. Add the basil and celery and cook, stirring, for another 2 minutes, then add the vinegar, sugar and tomato purée. Cook, stirring, for 2 minutes then add all the remaining ingredients except the parsley. Bring to a simmer and cook, stirring occasionally, for 15–20 minutes until the sauce has thickened and reduced and the flavours have mingled.

Stir the parsley into the caponata and spoon on to plates. Serve with Wet Polenta.

A Ukrainian speciality, pampushki come in a number of different varieties. This savoury version is an excellent, tasty way to use up leftover mashed potato; the raw grated pumpkin and potato create a wonderful crunchy contrast to the lovely, smooth mash and melted cheese. Be sure to use a winter pumpkin with dense, firm flesh here and not a watery Halloween lantern variety. A butternut squash will also work well.

PUMPKIN & POTATO PAMPUSHKI

SERVES 4–6

550g (1lb 2oz) potato, peeled
450g (14½oz) pumpkin or butternut
  squash, peeled and deseeded
olive oil
1 teaspoon finely chopped thyme
1 teaspoon finely chopped rosemary
gluten-free flour, for dusting (or regular
  flour, for non gluten-free)
salt and pepper

For the cheese filling
small knob of butter
1 teaspoon finely chopped rosemary
1 teaspoon finely chopped thyme
3 garlic cloves, finely chopped
150g (5oz) soft goats' cheese
1 tablespoon double cream, crème
  fraîche or soured cream

To serve
wilted spinach
Tomato & Basil Sauce (*see* page 151)

For the cheese filling, melt the butter in a saucepan, add the herbs and garlic and cook for 1 minute at a low heat. Tip into a bowl, crumble over the goats' cheese and mix well. Add the cream, season to taste and stir together until smooth. Cover with clingfilm and refrigerate.

Preheat the oven to 190°C/fan 170°C/Gas Mark 5. Cut 300g (10oz) of the potatoes into even-sized pieces and drop into a saucepan of water. Bring to the boil and cook for 15–20 minutes until tender. Drain. While still hot, mash the potatoes and tip into a bowl. Meanwhile, cut two-thirds of the pumpkin into even-sized chunks, put in a roasting pan with a drizzle of oil and roast for 25–30 minutes until very soft. Add to the bowl with the potato and mash together.

Using the large side of your grater, grate the remaining potato and pumpkin. Squeeze the grated vegetables with your hands to remove as much liquid as possible, then add to the mashed vegetables with the herbs and season with salt and pepper to taste. Mix together well.

Divide both the mashed vegetables and cheese filling into 4–6 portions, depending on the number you are serving, and roll into balls. Take a ball of mash and flatten it in your hand, place a portion of cheese filling in the centre and wrap the mash around it to cover completely. Coat the pampushki in flour, dusting off any excess.

Heat some oil in a large nonstick frying pan over a low heat. Add the pampushki and fry for 5 minutes on each side until golden brown and crunchy. Serve with wilted spinach and warm Tomato & Basil Sauce.

If you have an important meal which requires a centrepiece – Christmas dinner for example – look no further. Slightly sweet and not overpoweringly rich, the filling can be made in advance, with the Wellington assembled to bake later. While we like to make this vegan with the use of vegan puff pastry and soy cream to glaze, you can always use regular puff, brushing with a little beaten egg, instead. We serve this with Braised Red Cabbage, Maple-roasted Root Vegetables and Port Gravy (see pages 193, 188 and 236).

ROASTED PORTOBELLO MUSHROOM,
PECAN & CHESTNUT WELLINGTON

SERVES 8–10

light olive oil
1 large white onion, sliced
6 garlic cloves, finely chopped
1 tablespoon chopped rosemary
1 teaspoon chopped thyme
2 tablespoons white wine
1 teaspoon dark brown sugar
100g (3½oz) pecans
200g (7oz) cooked and peeled chestnuts
60g (2½oz) fresh white breadcrumbs
truffle oil, to taste
500g (1lb) vegan puff pastry
25ml (1fl oz) soy cream

For the roasted portobello mushrooms

500g (1lb) portobello mushrooms, trimmed
2 garlic cloves, sliced
1 thyme sprig, leaves picked
1 rosemary sprig, leaves picked
2–3 tablespoons olive oil

To serve

Braised Red Cabbage (*see* page 193)
Maple-roasted Root Vegetables (*see* page 188)
Port Gravy (*see* page 236)

Preheat the oven to 180°C/fan 160°C/Gas Mark 4. Line a baking tray with baking parchment.

To prepare the roasted portobello mushrooms, arrange the mushrooms on a baking tray, scatter with the garlic and herbs and drizzle over the olive oil. Roast for 10–15 minutes until the mushrooms are tender but still holding their shape. Remove from the oven and set aside.

Warm a splash of olive oil in a small heavy-based saucepan, add the onion, garlic and herbs and cook, stirring, for 15 minutes or until the onion is caramelized. Pour over the white wine, stir in the sugar to dissolve and cook for another 2–3 minutes. Remove from the heat and tip into a large mixing bowl.

Put the pecans and chestnuts in a food processor and pulse into small pieces. Add to the mixing bowl along with the breadcrumbs and mix everything together well.

Cut four of the portobello mushrooms in half and set aside (these will form the centre of your Wellington). Cut the remaining mushrooms into small chunks, add them to the mixing bowl and mix everything together carefully with your fingers. Finally add the truffle oil, a drop or two at a time, until you reach your desired strength of flavour.

Roll out the puff pastry onto a floured piece of baking parchment into a 20 x 35-cm (8 x 14-inch) rectangle around 3mm- (^{1}/$_8$-inch) thick. Trim the edges of the pastry to make it tidy and reserve the excess for decorating.

Spoon half the mushroom and nut mixture lengthways down the centre of the pastry and spread out evenly, leaving a border of 5–6cm (2–2^1/$_2$ inches) down the longer sides. Arrange the portobello halves over the mixture down the middle of the pastry then cover with the remainder of the mixture.

Brush the edges of the pastry with a little soy cream and fold over the ends and sides to roll the pastry around the filling. To do this, hold one side of the parchment and lift it so it starts to cover the filling. Peel the baking parchment back, leaving the pastry in place, then do the same with the other side. The pastry should overlap in the middle. Lift the Wellington on to the prepared baking tray, turning it over so that the seam is on the bottom. Brush with some more soy cream and use the trimmings to decorate with stars, leaf shapes or whatever takes your fancy.

Bake the Wellington for 1–1^1/$_4$ hours, until puffed up, golden brown and cooked through. Serve with Braised Red Cabbage, Maple-roasted Root Vegetables and Port Gravy.

A vegetarian version of a classic steak and ale pie, our mushroom pie has been on the menu for more than a decade. It has all the wet winter's day appeal of the original, and is served with Roast Potato Wedges (see page 187) and minty mushy peas for extra ballast.

WILD MUSHROOM & ALE PIES

MAKES 8 INDIVIDUAL PIES

70g (3oz) dried ceps
1kg (2lb) mixed mushrooms (such
  as chestnut or Portobello), trimmed,
  washed and quartered
rapeseed or light olive oil
4 small white onions, sliced
3 garlic cloves, finely chopped
1 tablespoon light brown sugar
3 thyme sprigs, finely chopped
3 rosemary sprigs, finely chopped
300ml (½ pint) brown ale
2½ tablespoons plain flour
1 tablespoon wholegrain mustard
50ml (2fl oz) dark soy sauce
2 pre-rolled vegan puff pastry sheets,
  thawed if frozen
soy cream, to glaze
pinch of dried basil
pinch of dried thyme

To serve
Roast Potato Wedges (*see* page 187)
minty mushy peas

Preheat the oven to 180°C/fan 160°C/Gas Mark 4. Line a baking tray with baking parchment.

Rinse the ceps in warm water and strain to remove any sand or grit, then put in a bowl and cover with boiling water. Soak for 15 minutes, then strain, setting aside the soaking water, and roughly chop.

Meanwhile, arrange the mushroom pieces on a baking tray, drizzle with oil and roast for 15 minutes, until just tender. Remove and set aside, adding any excess mushroom juices to the reserved cep water.

Heat a splash of oil in a large heavy-based saucepan. Add the onions and garlic and cook gently, stirring occasionally, for 10–12 minutes until the onions begin to caramelize. Add the sugar, thyme and rosemary and cook for a further 10 minutes until the onions are golden and sweet.

Pour over the ale, bring to a simmer and cook for 5–10 minutes or until the liquid is reduced by two-thirds. Sprinkle over the flour and stir it in until smooth, then gradually add the mushroom juices, mustard and soy sauce. Return to a simmer and cook, stirring frequently, for 20–25 minutes until thickened. Stir in the roasted mushrooms and ceps to heat them through. Keep warm.

While the pie mix is cooking, cut the pastry into 12-cm (5-inch) squares. Place on the prepared baking tray and brush with soy cream. Sprinkle over the herbs and bake for 20 minutes, until puffed and golden. Remove from the oven, let cool slightly, then arrange on serving plates. Cut a square from the top of each pastry, spoon the hot pie filling into the holes and replace the lids. Serve with Roast Potato Wedges and minty mushy peas.

A filling and flavourful main course packed full of bright colours to cheer up your autumn table. You can make the chilli in advance to cut down on the labour involved here, while if you can't find baby pumpkins you could always use the round bottom part of a butternut squash.

BLACK BEAN CHILLI FILLED BABY PUMPKINS
WITH TOASTED COCONUT RICE

SERVES 8

8 baby pumpkins or winter squash
light oil (such as rapeseed, groundnut
  or sunflower)

For the Black Bean Chilli
light oil
200g (7oz) pumpkin, cut into 2.5-cm
  (1-inch) cubes
1 courgette, cut into 2.5-cm (1-inch) cubes
1 white onion, finely diced
3 garlic cloves, finely chopped
2 celery sticks, finely diced
1 red chilli, trimmed and finely chopped
1 tablespoon chopped thyme leaves
3 tablespoons tomato purée
2 x 400g (13oz) cans chopped tomatoes
1 tablespoon dark brown sugar
½ cinnamon stick
2 chipotle chillies, roughly chopped or
  3 tablespoons chipotle chilli paste
½ teaspoon paprika
400ml (14fl oz) water
480g (15oz) canned black beans
1 small bunch of coriander leaves,
  chopped

For the Toasted Coconut Rice
light oil
2 green chillies, finely chopped
500g (1lb) basmati rice, washed
300ml (½ pint) water
40ml (1½fl oz) coconut milk
75g (3oz) desiccated coconut

Preheat the oven to 200°C/fan 180°C/Gas Mark 6.

For the black bean chilli, drizzle a little oil on to the base of a roasting tin. Add the pumpkin pieces and mix together thoroughly. Roast for 10 minutes, then add the courgette and cook for a further 5–10 minutes until the vegetables are tender. Set aside.

Heat a splash of oil in a large heavy-based saucepan, add the onion and cook gently, stirring, for 5 minutes, until softened and translucent. Add the garlic, celery, chilli and thyme and cook for another 10 minutes, then add the tomato purée, tomatoes, sugar, cinnamon, chillies, paprika and water and bring to a simmer. Cook for 20 minutes or so, stirring frequently, until the chilli has thickened and reduced. Add the beans and cook for a further 10 minutes, then stir in the roasted vegetables and coriander and keep warm.

Meanwhile, roast the baby pumpkins. Cut the top off each in a neat circle and scoop out the seeds with a spoon. Place on a baking tray, drizzle with a little oil and bake for 20–30 minutes until the flesh is cooked. Cover with tin foil to keep warm and set aside until needed.

For the toasted coconut rice, heat a drizzle of oil in a saucepan, add the chillies and cook, stirring, for 2 minutes. Add the rice and cook, stirring, for 2 minutes, then cover with the water. Bring to the boil and simmer for 10–12 minutes, until the water has evaporated and the rice is tender. Remove from the heat, pour over the coconut milk, and set aside, covered, for 5 minutes. Stir in the desiccated coconut to finish. To serve, place a large scoop of rice on each plate, fill the warm pumpkins with the chilli and place one on each plate beside the rice.

While traditionally this much-adapted Russian dish is made with beef, here we have changed the filling for a mixture of earthy mushrooms along with the rather unusual addition of lapsang souchong tea to give this dish a slightly smoky taste. Seeking out a variety of mushrooms including ceps, chestnut and field mushrooms will definitely help give the stroganoff more punch. We like to serve this with our Walnut & Leek Pilaf (see page 199).

LAPSANG-SCENTED MUSHROOM STROGANOFF

SERVES 6–8

1kg (2lb) mixed mushrooms
   (such as ceps, chestnut and field
   mushrooms), trimmed
light cooking oil (such as rapeseed,
   groundnut or sunflower)
2 lapsang souchong tea bags
600ml (1 pint) boiling water
30g (1oz) butter
2 onions, finely sliced
6 garlic cloves, very finely chopped
1 tablespoon smoked paprika
2 tablespoons corn flour
400ml (14fl oz) double cream
2 tablespoons Dijon mustard
2 tablespoons tomato purée
200g (7oz) soured cream
1 bunch of dill leaves, chopped
salt and pepper
Walnut & Leek Pilaf (*see* page 199),
   to serve

Preheat the oven to 190°C/fan 170°C/Gas Mark 5.

Cut the mushrooms into even, bite-sized pieces. Drizzle a little oil on to the base of a roasting tin, add the mushrooms and mix together thoroughly. Roast for 10–15 minutes, until the mushrooms are tender but have not yet begun to shrivel. Set aside.

Put the lapsang souchong tea bags in a bowl, cover with the boiling water and leave to infuse for 4 minutes. Remove and discard the tea bags and set the tea aside.

Melt the butter in a large saucepan over a medium heat, add the onions and cook, stirring, for 5 minutes until soft. Add the garlic and paprika and fry for another 2–3 minutes, then add the flour and stir together well. Pour over the tea and double cream and stir in the mushrooms, mustard and tomato purée. Bring to a simmer and cook gently for 15 minutes, stirring occasionally, until the sauce has begun to reduce and thicken slightly.

Add the soured cream and cook for a further 5 minutes until the stroganoff is thick and creamy. Season with salt and pepper to taste. Divide between serving plates, scatter over the chopped dill and serve with Walnut & Leek Pilaf.

A simple, classic dish which we've given a bit of a pimp with the addition of sun-blushed tomatoes, caramelized onions and a basil crumb topping. When cooking something this simple though it's the basics that really need looking after – try to use a really good cheese here and don't skimp on the pasta either, as you will be able to taste the difference.

MACARONI CHEESE WITH SUN-BLUSHED TOMATOES & BASIL CRUMB TOPPING

SERVES 8–10

500g (1lb) macaroni
olive oil
500g (1lb) white onions, sliced
2 teaspoons demerara sugar
220g (7½oz) fresh breadcrumbs
3 garlic cloves, very finely chopped
1 bunch of basil leaves, chopped
150g (5oz) sun-blushed tomatoes,
  chopped
salt and pepper

For the cheese sauce
1.5 litres (2½ pints) milk, plus extra
  if necessary
1 onion, sliced
3 bay leaves
100g (3½oz) butter, plus extra
  for greasing
150g (5oz) plain flour
200g (7oz) mature Cheddar cheese,
  grated
100g (3½oz) vegetarian Parmesan-style
  hard cheese

Preheat the oven to 190°C/fan 170°C/Gas Mark 5. Grease a 30 x 22-cm (12 x 9-inch) rectangular ovenproof dish. Bring a saucepan of salted water to the boil, add the macaroni and cook according to the packet instructions until al dente. Drain and set aside.

Heat a splash of oil in a saucepan over a medium heat, add the onions and cook, stirring occasionally, for 10–15 minutes until golden brown. Add the sugar, season with salt and pepper and cook for another 10 minutes or until the onions are dark golden. Remove from the heat.

Put the breadcrumbs, garlic and chopped basil into a food processor and blend together. Set aside.

For the cheese sauce, heat the milk in a saucepan over a medium–low heat, add the onion and bay leaves and bring to a simmer. Set aside for at least 10 minutes to allow the flavours to infuse. Melt the butter in a separate saucepan over a low heat, add the flour and stir together to make a roux. Using a strainer, gradually add the milk, stirring continuously with a whisk to avoid it becoming lumpy. Stir in the grated cheeses, which will melt and help thicken the sauce. If you feel the sauce is getting too thick, add another splash of milk to thin it out.

Pour the sauce into a large mixing bowl, add the cooked pasta, caramelized onions and chopped sun-blushed tomatoes and mix together well. Spoon into the prepared ovenproof dish, cover with the breadcrumb mixture and drizzle a little olive oil over the top. Bake in the oven for 20 minutes or until golden brown. Leave to cool for 10 minutes before serving.

if served without couscous

An underrated vegetable in our opinion, cauliflower is great for absorbing flavours while retaining a nice texture. If you can get it, romanesco cauliflower looks beautiful in this dish. This recipe was developed to accommodate people who don't eat onions or garlic, with the ginger, celery, carrot and chilli providing the base layers of flavour in their place. It's a good dish to make in advance as the flavours will deepen and develop.

CAULIFLOWER & GREEN OLIVE TAGINE

SERVES 6–8

1 large cauliflower, separated into small florets
light cooking oil (such as rapeseed, groundnut or sunflower)
2 celery sticks, trimmed and finely diced
5 carrots, cut into 3-cm (1½-inch) chunks
30g (1oz) fresh root ginger, peeled and finely chopped
2 red chillies, trimmed and finely chopped
2 teaspoons ground cumin
2 teaspoons paprika
½ teaspoon ground turmeric
pinch of cayenne pepper
½ teaspoon vegetable bouillon powder
3 x 400g (13oz) cans chopped tomatoes
800ml (1½ pints) water
150g (5oz) pitted green olives
2 preserved lemons, pips removed and finely sliced
1 teaspoon caster sugar
2 x 400g (13oz) cans chickpeas, drained and rinsed
1 bunch of coriander leaves, chopped
salt and pepper

To serve
Apricot & Pistachio Couscous (optional; *see* page 192)

Bring a saucepan of salted water to the boil, add the cauliflower florets and blanch for 2–3 minutes until just tender. Drain and set aside.

Heat a splash of oil in a large saucepan or casserole dish over a medium heat, add the celery, carrot, ginger and chilli and sauté for 5 minutes until the celery is beginning to soften. Add the spices and bouillon powder, lower the heat and cook, stirring, for a further few minutes before adding the chopped tomatoes, water, olives, preserved lemons, cauliflower and sugar. Bring to a simmer and leave to cook for 20 minutes, stirring occasionally. Add the chickpeas and cook for a further 10 minutes until the cauliflower is tender and all the flavours have come together. Season to taste with salt and pepper.

Remove from the heat and stir through the coriander. Serve with Apricot & Pistachio Couscous, if liked.

If you're not keen on cauliflower, this recipe also works well with large chunks of **roast aubergine** or, for a wintery version, **roast pumpkin**.

If you find the tagine too spicy, serve it with soy yogurt to cool it down.

BURGERS

At Mildreds we make a different vegetarian burger pretty much every day. We use a huge range of different seasonal vegetables, herbs, spices and beans, and regularly sell over a hundred burgers daily. Once a customer asked us what machine we use to make them; he didn't believe us when we told him all of our burgers are made by hand.

The main binding agent used in our burgers is a dried soy protein mix, Sos mix, which can be found in most health food stores. If you're finding this hard to get hold of, swap in another vegetarian sausage mix in its place.

This Mediterranean burger goes really well with our Vegan Basil Mayonnaise (see page 232), slices of ripe tomato, red onion, rocket leaves and, for an extra treat, melted slices of buffalo mozzarella.

ITALIAN TOMATO, AUBERGINE
& BLACK OLIVE BURGERS

MAKES 6–10 BURGERS

light olive oil or other light cooking oil (such as rapeseed, groundnut or sunflower)

1½ aubergines, cut into 3-cm (1¼-inch) cubes

1 white onion, finely diced

2 rosemary sprigs, leaves picked and finely chopped

4 garlic cloves, finely chopped

400g (13oz) can chopped tomatoes

125g (4oz) tomato purée

1 chilli, trimmed and finely chopped

1½ tablespoons caster sugar

1 bunch of basil leaves, chopped

150g (5oz) pitted black olives, chopped

600g (1¼lb) Sos mix, or other vegetarian dehydrated sausage mix

To serve

sourdough rolls, split and toasted

rocket leaves

tomato slices

red onion slices

Vegan Basil Mayonnaise (*see* page 232)

Carrot Relish (*see* page 237)

melted buffalo mozzarella cheese slices

Roast Potato Wedges (*see* page 187)

Preheat the oven to 200°C/fan 180°C/Gas Mark 5.

Drizzle a little oil on to the base of a roasting tray. Add the aubergine pieces and mix together thoroughly. Roast for 15 minutes, or until the aubergine is cooked through but not mushy. Set aside to cool.

Once cool, tip the aubergine into a large mixing bowl, add all the other ingredients and, using your hands, knead for 5 minutes until everything is combined together. Cover with clingfilm, transfer to the refrigerator and leave to rest for 15 minutes.

Once rested, divide the mix into 6–10 even-sized pieces. (You may find at this point that the mix is too solid to divide easily – if so, simply add a little water to the mix, making sure that you stir it through thoroughly.) Shape the pieces into circular patties around 2–2.5cm (¾–1 inch) thick.

Heat a splash of oil in a large frying pan. When hot, add the patties and fry for 10 minutes on each side.

Pop the burgers into toasted sourdough rolls and stuff with rocket, tomato and red onion slices, Vegan Basil Mayonnaise, Carrot Relish and melted buffalo mozzarella, as you prefer. Serve with Roast Potato Wedges.

These always sell really fast when we put them on the menu – lots of chunky colourful vegetables and beans make for a great looking burger which pairs really well with guacamole, slices of fresh avocado and our Sweet Potato Fries (see page 186).

MEXICAN KIDNEY BEAN, JALAPEÑO, ROASTED PEPPER & SWEETCORN BURGERS

MAKES 6–10 BURGERS

300g (10oz) canned kidney beans, drained and rinsed
2 roasted red peppers in oil, drained and roughly chopped
100g (3½oz) sweetcorn kernels
4 spring onions, trimmed and roughly chopped
1 bunch of coriander leaves, roughly chopped
150g (5oz) jarred jalapeño chillies, drained and roughly chopped
400g (13oz) can chopped tomatoes
1 tablespoon smoked paprika
1 teaspoon ground coriander
½ teaspoon chilli powder
600g (1¼lb) Sos mix, or other vegetarian sausage mix
100–200ml (3½–7fl oz) water
light olive oil or other light cooking oil (such as rapeseed, groundnut or sunflower)

To serve
sourdough rolls, split and toasted
Guacamole (*see* page 175)
avocado slices
rocket leaves
tomato slices
red onion slices
Vegan Basil Mayonnaise (*see* page 232)
Carrot Relish (*see* page 237)
Sweet Potato Fries (*see* page 186)

Place all the solid ingredients in a large mixing bowl with 100ml (3½fl oz) water. Knead together with your hands until the beans have broken up and the mixture has come together. Continue to knead, adding more water if necessary, until the mixture is dense but pliable. Cover with clingfilm, transfer to the refrigerator and leave to rest for 20 minutes.

Once rested, divide the mix into 6–10 even-sized pieces. (You may find at this point the mix is too solid to divide easily – if so, simply add a little more water to the mix, making sure to stir it through thoroughly.) Shape the pieces into circular patties around 2–2.5cm (¾–1 inch) thick.

Heat a splash of oil in a large frying pan. When hot, add the patties and fry for 10 minutes on each side.

Pop the burgers into toasted sourdough rolls and stuff with Guacamole and avocado slices, or our usual combination of rocket, tomato and red onion slices, Vegan Basil Mayonnaise and Carrot Relish, as you prefer. Serve with Sweet Potato Fries.

A lovely purple burger with eastern European flavours, this is a consistent favourite at Mildreds and goes brilliantly with our Beer-battered Onion Rings (see page 194). We serve all our burgers with rocket, tomatoes, red onion, Vegan Basil Mayonnaise (see page 232) and Carrot Relish (see page 237) but you could go full on eastern European with these and serve them with sauerkraut or sour pickles instead.

BEETROOT, FENNEL, APPLE & DILL BURGERS

MAKES 6–10 BURGERS

3 small or 2 medium beetroot, peeled and coarsely grated
2 dessert apples, coarsely grated
1 fennel bulb, trimmed and finely chopped
1 bunch of dill leaves, chopped
1 tablespoon fennel seeds, toasted and lightly ground
600g (1¼lb) Sos mix, or other vegetarian sausage mix
450ml (¾ pint) water, plus extra if necessary
light olive oil or other light cooking oil (such as rapeseed, groundnut or sunflower)

To serve
sourdough rolls, split and toasted
rocket leaves
tomato slices
red onion slices
Vegan Basil Mayonnaise (*see* page 232)
Carrot Relish (*see* page 237)
Beer-battered Onion Rings (*see* page 194)

To make the burgers, combine all the ingredients except the oil in a large mixing bowl and knead together with your hands for 5 minutes to form a dense but pliable burger mixture. Cover with clingfilm, transfer to the refrigerator and leave to rest for 15 minutes.

Once rested, divide the mix into 6–10 even-sized pieces. (You may find at this point the mix is too solid to divide easily – if so, simply add a little more water to the mix, making sure to stir it through thoroughly.) Shape the pieces into circular patties around 2–2.5cm (¾–1 inch) thick.

Heat a splash of oil in a large frying pan. When hot, add the patties and fry for 10 minutes on each side.

Pop the burgers into toasted sourdough rolls and stuff with rocket, tomato and red onion slices, Vegan Basil Mayonnaise and Carrot Relish, as you prefer. Serve accompanied by Beer-battered Onion Rings.

PASTA

Pasta, sadly, is often the only vegetarian option offered by a lot of mainstream restaurants, so we weren't sure whether to include pasta recipes in this book. However, our daily pasta specials are so popular that we couldn't resist. Who doesn't love a delicious plate of this multifaceted carbohydrate (especially now that there are so many good gluten-free options for those people who had to avoid it previously)?

There are so many pasta sauces to choose from that we had a hard time narrowing it down. In the end, we've tried to include a bit of everything, from a simple Tomato & Basil Sauce (*see* page 151) that's perfect as a base (and great for sneaking vegetables onto picky children's plates), to summery Saffron & Goats' Cheese Sauce (*see* page 148) and wintery Creamy Mushroom & Sherry Vinegar Sauce (see page 146)... and more. We've recommended pasta varieties to accompany the sauces but feel free to experiment and find your own favourites.

Sherry vinegar might seem like a strange thing to add to a cream sauce but trust us, it gives it a sweet, rich flavour that sets the whole thing off perfectly. While lovely with orecchiette, the 'little ear' shaped pasta, it also pairs very well with potato gnocchi – just add a bottle of full-bodied red wine and some herby focaccia to mop up any leftover sauce for a deliciously rich, hearty meal.

CREAMY MUSHROOM & SHERRY VINEGAR ORECCHIETTE WITH FRENCH BEANS

SERVES 4–6

500g (1lb) orecchiette
200g (7oz) French beans, trimmed
 and cut in half

*For the Creamy Mushroom
& Sherry Vinegar Sauce*
500g (1lb) chestnut mushrooms,
 quartered
light cooking oil (such as rapeseed,
 groundnut or sunflower)
50g (2oz) dried ceps
25g (1oz) butter
4 garlic cloves, finely sliced
1 large white onion, finely sliced
1 tablespoon demerara sugar
handful of thyme sprigs, leaves picked
75ml (3fl oz) sherry vinegar
500ml (17fl oz) double cream
salt and pepper

Preheat the oven to 190°C/fan 170°C/Gas Mark 5. For the sauce, arrange the chestnut mushrooms on a baking tray, drizzle with a little oil and roast for 10–12 minutes until cooked but still firm. Remove from the oven and set aside. Rinse the ceps in warm water and strain to remove any sand or grit, then put in a bowl and cover with boiling water. Leave to soak for 15 minutes, then strain, setting aside the soaking water, and roughly chop.

Melt the butter in a saucepan over a medium heat, add the garlic and onion and sauté for 5–8 minutes, stirring frequently, until the onion has softened and is starting to caramelize. Add the sugar and thyme and continue to cook for 10–15 minutes until the onion is a golden brown.

Strain any liquid that has escaped from the chestnut mushrooms while roasting and add it to the onions along with the ceps, cep soaking water and sherry vinegar. Bring to a simmer and cook for about 10–15 minutes, until the liquid has almost entirely evaporated. Add the cream and simmer gently for a further 10–15 minutes until the sauce has thickened and reduced and is a deep caramel colour.

Meanwhile, cook the pasta and beans. Bring a small saucepan of salted water to the boil, add the beans and cook for 3–4 minutes until tender. Bring a separate saucepan of salted water to the boil, add the orecchiette and cook according to the packet instructions. Drain. Stir the chestnut mushrooms through the sauce and warm for a minute. Season the sauce to taste with salt and pepper, tip over the cooked pasta and beans and mix everything together well. Serve.

With its broad leaves, pretty little white flowers and unmistakeable garlicky aroma, wild garlic is a great seasonal food that grows happily in shady areas in deserted rural spots and urban parks alike. If you do find some in the wild, don't pick everything you see; just take a few leaves from several different plants so that they can recover. Wild garlic is now available in season at many good greengrocers and speciality food stores, though if you are struggling to get your hands on it, you can always use rocket here instead for a punchier, peppery alternative. Trofie is a little twisted pasta traditionally served with pesto. If you can't get hold of any then fusilli works well here too.

TROFIE WITH WILD GARLIC PESTO

SERVES 4–6

500g (1lb) trofie or fusilli

For the Wild Garlic Pesto
75g (3oz) wild garlic leaves
1 bunch of basil leaves
½ bunch of flat leaf parsley leaves
250ml (8fl oz) light olive oil
1 teaspoon sea salt flakes
pinch of black pepper
25g (1oz) vegetarian Parmesan-style
  hard cheese, grated
20g (¾oz) pine nuts, toasted

Bring a pan of salted water to the boil, add the pasta and cook according to the packet instructions.

While the pasta is cooking, make the wild garlic pesto. Wash the wild garlic leaves thoroughly and pat dry with a clean tea towel. Put them, along with the herbs, in a food processor, add a splash of the oil and blend briefly together.

Add the sea salt flakes, pepper, cheese and pine nuts and blend together, gradually adding the remaining olive oil until smooth. Taste and adjust the seasoning if necessary, then mix through the warm pasta. Serve.

This is a creamy, vibrant pasta dish that's perfect for a summer's lunch, with the thin courgette ribbons cooked briefly in the heat of the pasta and sauce. We like to use both yellow and green courgettes here to give the dish a bit of extra colour, but if you can't find the yellow ones then just green will do fine. The saffron in the sauce adds a lovely golden colour and a light, fragrant flavour that complements the goats' cheese, but again this can be left out if you don't have any to hand – just add a teaspoon of picked thyme leaves instead.

SAFFRON & GOATS' CHEESE TAGLIATELLE
WITH COURGETTES, CHERRY TOMATOES & BLACK OLIVES

SERVES 4–6

500g (1lb) fresh tagliatelle

**For the Saffron & Goats'
Cheese Sauce**
25g (1oz) butter
1 red chilli, deseeded and finely
  chopped
3–4 garlic cloves, finely chopped
finely grated rind and juice of ½ lemon
200ml (7fl oz) white wine
large pinch of saffron threads
1 teaspoon caster sugar
5 bay leaves
350g (11½oz) goats' cheese
700ml (1¼ pints) double cream
5 courgettes (3 green and 2 yellow),
  cut into thin ribbons using a French
  peeler or mandolin
200g (7oz) good-quality pitted black
  olives
300g (10oz) cherry tomatoes, quartered
salt and white pepper

To make the sauce, melt the butter in a saucepan over a medium heat, add the chilli, garlic and grated lemon rind and cook, stirring, for 3–4 minutes until the garlic has softened and is fragrant. Add the lemon juice, white wine, saffron, sugar and bay leaves, bring to a simmer and cook, stirring occasionally, for 10–15 minutes or until the liquid has reduced by half.

Remove any rind from the goats' cheese and crumble into pieces. Stir it into the sauce along with the cream and simmer gently for 5–10 minutes, stirring frequently, until the sauce has thickened and all the goats' cheese has dissolved evenly into the sauce. Season to taste with salt and white pepper.

Meanwhile, bring a saucepan of salted water to the boil and cook the pasta according to the instructions on the packet.

Stir the courgettes, olives and tomatoes into the sauce, add the cooked pasta and mix everything together well. Remove from the heat and serve.

This smooth, sweet sauce is great served with our Saffron & Pea Risotto Cakes (see page 111) but is also excellent stirred through pasta. While other roasted red peppers can be used, we love the sweet finish that Spanish piquillo peppers lend to the sauce, so do try and hunt them down if you can.

PENNE WITH RED PEPPER SAUCE

SERVES 4–6

16 asparagus spears, trimmed
250g (8oz) peas, defrosted if frozen
500g (1lb) penne
salt
200g (7oz) grated vegetarian
  Parmesan-style hard cheese, to serve

For the Red Pepper Sauce
3 tablespoons light olive oil
1 onion, diced
2 garlic cloves, crushed
1 celery stick, trimmed and diced
1 carrot, grated
200g (7oz) canned plum tomatoes
300g (10oz) roasted piquillo peppers
  in oil, drained
1 teaspoon caster sugar
1 teaspoon salt
1 teaspoon tomato purée
pinch of black pepper
300ml (½ pint) double cream, plus
  extra if needed

Bring a saucepan of salted water to the boil. Break the woody ends off the asparagus spears and cut each into 2–3 pieces. Blanch for a minute, then add the peas and continue to blanch for a further 20 seconds. Drain and rinse under cold water to refresh. Set aside.

For the red pepper sauce, heat the olive oil in a saucepan over a medium heat, add the onion, garlic, celery and carrot and cook for 5 minutes, stirring, until the onion is starting to soften. Add all the remaining ingredients except the double cream, bring to a simmer, and leave to cook gently, stirring occasionally, for 20 minutes until thickened and reduced. Stir in the double cream and continue to simmer gently for a further 15–20 minutes until thick and creamy.

Remove the sauce from the heat and blend with a stick blender or in a food processor until smooth. If the sauce is looking a little thick, add an extra splash of double cream. Return the sauce to the saucepan and keep warm.

Bring a saucepan of salted water to the boil and cook the pasta according to the packet instructions. Drain and add to the sauce along with the blanched asparagus and peas and mix together well. Divide between bowls and scatter over the grated Parmesan to serve.

Our resident Italian chef, Alex Aimassi, taught us this recipe and, while we had never put such a lot of different vegetables into a tomato sauce before, we have to admit it is undoubtedly much improved in both depth of flavour and texture. The sweetness of the sauce contrasts well with the salty tapenade, with the roasted aubergines and baby spinach adding a wonderful splash of colour.

RIGATONI WITH TOMATO & BASIL SAUCE
& BLACK OLIVE TAPENADE

SERVES 4–6

4 large aubergines
light olive oil
500g (1lb) rigatoni
75g (3oz) baby spinach leaves
salt
200g (7oz) grated vegetarian
 Parmesan-style hard cheese, to serve

For the Tomato & Basil Sauce
light olive oil
1 onion, diced
2 garlic cloves, very finely chopped
1 celery stick, diced
1 carrot, grated
1 bunch of basil
½ small red chilli, trimmed, deseeded
 and diced
2 x 400g (13oz) cans plum tomatoes
1 teaspoon caster sugar
200ml (7fl oz) water
salt and pepper

For the Black Olive Tapenade
200g (7oz) pitted kalamata olives
large handful of parsley, chopped
2 garlic cloves, crushed
60ml (2½fl oz) olive oil
juice of ½ lemon
30g (1¼oz) capers in brine, drained
 and rinsed

To make the black olive tapenade, put all the ingredients into a food processor and blend to a smooth paste. Set aside until needed.

For the sauce, heat a splash of olive oil in a large saucepan over a medium heat, add the onion, garlic, celery, carrot, basil and chilli and cook, stirring, for about 8 minutes until the onions are softened and lightly coloured. Add the canned plum tomatoes, sugar and water and season with salt and pepper. Bring to a simmer and cook gently, stirring occasionally, for 25–30 minutes until the sauce has thickened and reduced by half.

Meanwhile, preheat the oven to 180°C/fan 160°C/Gas Mark 4. Cut the aubergines into 2.5-cm (1-inch) cubes and rinse under running water. Drain well and place on a baking tray with a drizzle of olive oil, season with salt and mix together well. Roast for 15 minutes, until the aubergines are golden and cooked through. Set aside.

Remove the sauce from the heat and blend with a stick blender or in a food processor until smooth. Return to the pan and keep warm.

Bring a saucepan of salted water to the boil and cook the pasta according to the packet instructions. Drain the pasta, add it to the sauce with the aubergines and baby spinach leaves and mix together well. Divide between bowls, drizzle over the tapenade and scatter with the grated Parmesan to serve.

This recipe is all about the sauce. The recipe here will make about three times the amount you need for this stir-fry. This is no bad thing, however, as the sauce is exceptionally tasty and can be easily frozen in portions for later use. Simply pop it in freezer bags or use it to fill an ice cube tray and you'll have a sauce ready to whip up a delicious, authentic stir-fry at a moment's notice. You can really use any vegetables you like for this dish and, if you're really pushed for time, even the pre-prepared stir-fry mix you can buy in the supermarkets will work fine.

SHIITAKE MUSHROOM & CHINESE VEGETABLE STIR-FRY

SERVES 4–6

vegetable oil
4 carrots, sliced thinly into discs
12 baby corn, left whole or sliced in half
1 red pepper, cored, deseeded and sliced
1 red chilli, trimmed and finely diced
4 garlic cloves, very finely chopped
350g (11½oz) choy sum (Chinese flowering cabbage), shredded
350g (11½oz) Chinese leaf cabbage, shredded
5 spring onions, trimmed and sliced into 5-cm (2-inch) batons
steamed jasmine rice, to serve

For the shiitake mushroom sauce
light cooking oil (such as rapeseed, groundnut or sunflower)
100g (3½oz) shiitake mushrooms, trimmed
100ml (3½fl oz) shaoxing rice wine or sherry
50ml (2fl oz) light soy sauce
50ml (2fl oz) kecap manis (sweet soy sauce)
1 star anise
300ml (½ pint) water
1 tablespoon cornflour

For the shiitake mushroom sauce, heat a drizzle of oil in a saucepan, add the mushrooms and cook for 3–5 minutes, stirring, until soft. Deglaze the pan with the rice wine, then add the soy sauce, kecap manis, star anise and water and bring to a simmer. Continue to cook, stirring occasionally, for 10–15 minutes or until reduced by a third, then remove from the heat and purée with a stick blender or in a food processor until smooth.

Return the sauce to the pan. Mix the cornflour with a few tablespoons of water, add to the sauce and cook for 3–5 minutes, stirring frequently, until thickened. Remove from the heat and set aside.

Heat a wok over a high heat, add a splash of vegetable oil and stir-fry the carrots, baby corn and pepper for 2 minutes, adding a splash of water along the way to steam the vegetables slightly. Add the chilli, garlic, choy sum and Chinese leaf cabbage and stir-fry for 2 minutes more, adding a further splash of water if necessary. Add the spring onions and 100ml (3½fl oz) of the shiitake sauce and cook, stirring, for a few minutes until the sauce coats the ingredients evenly. Serve with fragrant jasmine rice.

This vegetarian version of a traditional beef pho – the famous dish from the north of Vietnam – is a delicious, fragrant noodle and vegetable broth topped with bean sprouts and mint. If you're not keen on mushroom or seaweed this will still work without them; substitute any vegetables you like. Vietnamese mint is different from regular garden mint as it is stronger and has a more peppery taste. You can find it in Asian supermarkets and good greengrocers, though if you can't get hold of it, garden mint makes a suitable substitute.

SHIITAKE MUSHROOM & SEAWEED PHO

SERVES 6–8

2 large white onions, unpeeled

15-cm (6-inch) piece of fresh root ginger

3 tablespoons sesame oil

1 red chilli, roughly chopped

3 garlic cloves

5 shiitake mushrooms, trimmed

finely grated rind of ½ orange and juice
  of 2 oranges

2 tablespoons tamarind paste

6 star anise

1 cinnamon stick

2 litres (3½ pints) water

100ml (3½fl oz) tamari

100ml (3½fl oz) maple syrup

2 nori seaweed sheets, cut into strips,
  or 50g (2oz) dried kelp soaked in
  300ml (½ pint) hot water

To finish

3 tablespoons sesame oil

10 shiitake mushrooms, trimmed and
  thinly sliced

1 red chilli, trimmed and thinly sliced,
  plus extra to garnish

300g (10oz) wild rice noodles

500g (1lb) bean sprouts

2 handfuls of coriander leaves

2 handfuls of Vietnamese mint leaves

2 nori seaweed sheets, cut into thin
  strips

Add the whole onions and ginger to a hot griddle pan or barbecue and cook for 10–15 minutes, turning occasionally, until the onion and ginger skins have blackened and the onions have softened and caramelized. Set aside to cool, then peel off the skins and cut into large chunks.

Warm the sesame oil in a large saucepan over a medium heat, add the onion, ginger, chilli, whole garlic cloves, shiitake mushrooms and grated orange rind and sauté for 5–10 minutes until the mixture is fragrant and the flavours have melded together. Add the orange juice, tamarind paste, star anise and cinnamon and cook, stirring, for a few more minutes, then stir in the water, tamari and maple syrup and bring to the boil. Reduce the heat and simmer gently for 20 minutes, or until the liquid has reduced by about a half. Strain into a bowl and add the nori seaweed or soaked kelp.

To finish, return the pan to the heat with the sesame oil, add the shiitake mushrooms and chilli and cook for 2–3 minutes until the mushrooms are warmed through.

Return the strained broth to the pan and bring to a simmer. Add the rice noodles and cook for 3–5 minutes, until the noodles are just cooked. Ladle into bowls and scatter over the bean sprouts, herbs, nori seaweed strips and a few extra chilli slices. Serve.

The smoked tofu ragu used here is rich and full of deep, complex flavours that contrast well with the creamy béchamel and tangy feta cheese.

AUBERGINE MOUSSAKA WITH SMOKED TOFU RAGU

SERVES 8–10

1.5kg (3lb) aubergine, cut into 5-mm (¼-inch) rounds
225g (7½oz) smoked tofu, crumbled
½ teaspoon fennel seeds
½ teaspoon cumin seeds
½ teaspoon smoked paprika
½ teaspoon vegetable bouillon powder
½ tablespoon chilli oil
50g (2oz) feta cheese
salt

For the tomato sauce
splash of light cooking oil
1 white onion, finely diced
3 garlic cloves
1 carrot, finely diced
½ small leek, trimmed, cleaned and diced
½ red chilli, trimmed and finely diced
½ fennel bulb, trimmed and finely diced
600g (1¼lb) chopped tomatoes
1½ tablespoons tomato purée
250ml (8fl oz) water
1½ tablespoons caster sugar
½ cinnamon stick

For the béchamel sauce
500ml (17fl oz) milk
pinch of grated nutmeg
¼ white onion
1 bay leaf
pinch of white pepper
35g (1½oz) butter, plus extra for greasing
40g (1½oz) plain flour

To garnish
handful of fresh mint leaves, chopped
2 red chillies, chopped

Preheat the oven to 180°C/fan 160°C/Gas Mark 4. Grease a 30 x 22-cm (12 x 9-inch) rectangular ovenproof dish with butter. Sprinkle the aubergines with salt and leave to stand in a colander set over a bowl for 20 minutes. Meanwhile, mix the tofu in a bowl with the spices, bouillon powder and chilli oil. Spread across a baking tray and roast for 20 minutes, turning the tofu a few times during cooking, until it begins to crisp. Rinse the aubergines and arrange on oiled baking trays. Roast for 8 minutes on each side or until soft. Remove from the oven and reduce the heat to 160°C/fan 140°C/Gas Mark 3.

For the tomato sauce, heat the oil in a saucepan over a low heat, add the onion and garlic and cook, stirring, for 8–10 minutes until translucent. Add the carrot, leek, chilli and fennel and cook for a further 5 minutes until beginning to soften. Add the tomatoes, purée, water, sugar and cinnamon and simmer gently for 20 minutes, stirring occasionally. Leave to cool then stir in the roasted tofu and set aside.

Meanwhile, make the béchamel. Heat the milk in a saucepan, add the nutmeg, onion, bay leaf and pepper, bring to a simmer and remove from the heat. Set aside for at least 10 minutes to allow the flavours to infuse. Melt the butter in another saucepan, add the flour and stir together. Using a strainer, gradually add the milk, stirring continuously with a whisk to avoid it becoming lumpy. Continue to stir, over a low heat, until the sauce is thick, glossy and custard-like.

To assemble, arrange one-third of the aubergines on the base of the prepared dish. Spoon over half the tofu and tomato sauce, then add a second layer of aubergines and the remaining tofu sauce. Layer over the remaining aubergines and cover with the béchamel. Crumble over the feta and bake for 45 minutes until bubbling and the top is lightly brown. If the moussaka looks like it is colouring too quickly, cover it with foil to stop it from burning. Remove from the oven and leave to cool for 10 minutes. Garnish with chopped mint and chilli and serve.

Mee Goreng is a spicy, dry stir-fried noodle dish found in Malaysia, Indonesia and Singapore. Here's our vegetarian version. We use a couple of ingredients which you might not be familiar with; kecap manis is a thick, sweet Indonesian soy sauce that is widely available in Asian supermarkets. It is key to the flavour of this dish so we urge you to seek it out, though you could substitute hoisin sauce (just add half the quantity). Kai lan is also known as Chinese broccoli or Chinese kale, and has a similar flavour to broccoli. If you struggle to find it use Tenderstem broccoli instead. For best results and to avoid the stir-fry releasing too much liquid, cook in two batches.

MEE GORENG

SERVES 4–6

vegetable oil
4 eggs, lightly beaten
1 onion, sliced
6 garlic cloves, very finely chopped
40g (1½oz) fresh root ginger, peeled
  and very finely chopped
1 red chilli, trimmed and finely diced
2 yellow peppers, cored, deseeded
  and diced
600g (1¼lb) kai lan (Chinese broccoli) or
  choy sum (Chinese cabbage), shredded
3 carrots, halved and finely sliced
1 teaspoon chilli flakes or sambal paste
1 teaspoon ground coriander
1 teaspoon ground cumin
1 x 500g (1lb) packet of cooked
  egg noodles
4 spring onions, trimmed and sliced
300g (10oz) bean sprouts
60ml (2½fl oz) dark soy sauce
120ml (4fl oz) kecap manis
  (sweet soy sauce)

To garnish
4 limes, cut into wedges
200g (7oz) roasted peanuts
handful of fresh coriander leaves

In a medium-sized frying pan heat a splash of oil, pour in the beaten eggs, quickly stir and shake the pan to distribute them evenly. Cook until set. Slip the omelette on to a plate, roll up into a large cigar shape and slice into strips. Set to one side.

Heat a large wok or frying pan over a high heat until very hot, then add a splash of oil, swirling to coat the surface evenly. Add the onion and stir-fry for 2–3 minutes until just beginning to colour, then add the garlic, ginger, chilli, peppers, kai lan, carrots and a splash of water and stir-fry for another 2–3 minutes, until the vegetables are just tender.

Add the chilli flakes, ground coriander and cumin and stir-fry for 20–30 seconds, adding another splash of water to stop them from burning. Add the noodles, spring onions and bean sprouts and stir in the soy sauce and kecap manis. Spoon on to serving plates, top with the omelette slices and garnish with lime wedges, roasted peanuts and fresh coriander leaves.

LATIN

At Mildreds we are passionate about Latin food. Here we've put together a great spread of Latin treats, taking influences from Argentina, Chile, Mexico and Peru among other countries. Fresh, spicy and zesty – this is perfect party food that is great fun to make and eat.

Whereas the other salads in this book can all be served as starters or main courses, this is really intended as an accompaniment to Mexican or Latin dishes like our Black Bean and Pumpkin Burritos (see page 165). Fresh, crunchy and slightly spicy, it works well as a side – though if you did want to make it more substantial just add some grated cheese and a few handfuls of tortilla chips.

MEXICAN SALAD WITH AVOCADO, BABY GEM, SPRING ONION & JALAPEÑO

SERVES 6–8 AS A SIDE DISH

6 baby gem lettuces, trimmed
2 large ripe avocados, sliced or just
 scooped out into chunks with a spoon
3 jalapeño chillies, sliced
200g (7oz) red cherry tomatoes, sliced
 in half
200g (7oz) yellow cherry tomatoes,
 sliced in half
6 spring onions, trimmed and finely
 sliced diagonally
handful of coriander leaves
100ml (3½fl oz) Chipotle Lime Dressing
 (*see* page 240)

Separate the lettuce leaves and place in a large bowl along with all the remaining ingredients. Toss together well to mix and serve on plates alongside a main dish.

While Mexican ingredients are easier to get hold of these days, you may have trouble finding some of the items below in your local supermarket. A quick look online for a specialist supplier like the Cool Chile Company will help root out the more unusual ones. Likewise, if you can't find dried chipotle, just use regular chilli flakes instead. This is great served with Guacamole (see page 175) and Tomatillo Rice (see page 198).

BLACK BEAN & PUMPKIN BURRITOS

SERVES 6–8

light cooking oil
400g (13oz) pumpkin or butternut
  squash, peeled, deseeded and cut into
  2.5-cm (1-inch) chunks
300g (10oz) dried black turtle beans
1 teaspoon chopped epazote
1 litre (1¾ pints) water
½ teaspoon bicarbonate of soda
1 onion, finely diced
1 red pepper, cored, deseeded and sliced
3 garlic cloves, very finely chopped
¼ teaspoon cayenne pepper
1 teaspoon paprika
1 teaspoon smoked paprika
2 teaspoons ground cumin
1 teaspoon crushed dried chipotle chilli
  or dried hot chilli flakes
400g (13oz) can chopped tomatoes
2 tablespoons tomato purée
200g (7oz) sweetcorn kernels
275g (9oz) Cheddar cheese, grated
6–8 flour tortillas
salt

To serve
shredded iceburg lettuce
Pico de Gallo (*see* page 22)
soured cream

Preheat the oven to 190°C/fan 170°C/Gas Mark 5. Drizzle a little oil on to the base of a roasting tin. Add the pumpkin pieces, season with salt and mix together thoroughly. Roast for 15 minutes, until cooked through. Set aside.

Meanwhile, place the beans, epazote, water and bicarbonate of soda in a medium saucepan and bring to a simmer. Cook, stirring occasionally to stop the beans sticking to the bottom of the pan, for 30–40 minutes, until the beans have begun to break down and become mushy.

Heat a splash of oil in a separate saucepan, add the onion and sauté for 5 minutes until the onion begins to colour. Add the pepper and garlic and cook for another 2–3 minutes, then add the cayenne pepper, paprikas, cumin and chilli and cook over a low heat for a few minutes to release their flavours, being careful not to let them burn. Add the chopped tomatoes, tomato purée and sweetcorn and season with salt. Bring to a simmer, then lower the heat and cook gently, stirring occasionally, for 25–30 minutes, until the sauce has thickened and reduced and the flavours have melded together.

Stir the pumpkin and beans into the sauce and heat gently to warm through. Remove from the heat. Divide the black bean and pumpkin chilli between the tortillas, roll them tightly, cover in the cheese and place under a hot grill for 2–3 minutes, until the cheese has melted. Serve with shredded iceberg lettuce, *Pico de Gallo* and soured cream.

Brie may not be the first cheese that springs to mind when you think of quesadillas but it does work fantastically well at sandwiching the tortillas together. These are great served as a starter with a little Guacamole (see page 175) and soured cream, or as something to snack on for a party. If you can't get your hands on Mexican oregano then just use normal oregano instead.

MANGO, BRIE & JALAPEÑO QUESADILLAS

MAKES 6 QUESADILLAS

1 mango, peeled and finely diced
160g (5½oz) Brie, sliced
¼ teaspoon dried Mexican oregano
1 small jalapeño chilli, trimmed
 and diced
6 x 15-cm (6-inch) tortillas
Guacamole (*see* page 175), to serve

Mix the mango, Brie, oregano and chilli together in a bowl.

Lay the tortillas out on a flat work surface and fill one half of each with a generous tablespoon of the filling mixture. Fold the tortillas in half, pressing down on them gently with your fingertips to ensure they hold their shape during cooking.

Heat a frying pan or griddle pan over a medium heat, add the quesadillas and cook for 1–2 minutes on each side until they are golden brown and the cheese has started to melt. Serve with Guacamole.

A good alternative to Brie would be **smoked cheddar** or **mozzarella cheese**.

Empanadas are to Latin America what pasties are to Cornwall, and can be found almost everywhere. Typical vegetarian versions feature a mix of cheese and spinach or sweet potato but we like to load ours with a variety of cheeses. These are delicious served with Pebre (see page 176), the tang of the tomato and vinegar acting as the perfect foil to the rich, cheesy, flaky empanadas. The calorie count of these empanadas can be brought down slightly by oven baking rather than deep-frying, just note that you will need to make the dough a little thicker if doing so.

TRIPLE CHEESE EMPANADAS

MAKES 20 FRIED OR 15 BAKED EMPANADAS

150g (5oz) diced mozzarella cheese
150g (5oz) grated mature Cheddar cheese
150g (5oz) grated smoked Cheddar cheese
8 spring onions, trimmed and finely chopped
2 red chillies, trimmed and finely chopped
beaten egg, to glaze
1 litre (1¾ pints) sunflower oil, for deep-frying (optional)

For the dough
250g (8oz) plain flour, plus extra for dusting
40g (1½oz) butter
1 teaspoon salt
½ teaspoon baking powder
½ teaspoon baking soda
1 tablespoon caster sugar
½ teaspoon ground turmeric
½ teaspoon chilli powder
170ml (6fl oz) milk
110ml (3½fl oz) water

For the dough, mix together all the solid ingredients in a bowl. Heat the milk and water together to just below boiling point, then remove from the heat and stir into the mixture to form a dough. Leave to cool. Once cool, knead the dough until it is smooth and elastic, cover it with clingfilm and leave it to rest in the refrigerator for at least 30 minutes.

Mix together the cheeses, spring onions and chillies well in a bowl.

Once rested, separate the dough into 20 balls for frying or 15 balls for baking. Roll out the dough on a lightly floured surface into circles around 25cm (10 inches) in diameter. Brush the edges with beaten egg, place a tablespoon of filling in the centre of each and fold them together to make a half moon shape. Finally press the edges together with a fork to make sure they are well sealed and there are no weak points where the cheese can escape.

Depending on whether you are deep-frying or baking your empanadas, either fill a large saucepan or deep-fryer with the sunflower oil and heat to 180°C (350°F), or until a cube of bread thrown into the oil browns in 30 seconds, or preheat the oven to 190°C/fan 170°C/Gas Mark 5.

Deep-fry the empanadas for 3–5 minutes until lightly golden, remove with a slotted spoon and drain on kitchen paper. Alternatively bake the empanadas for 15–20 minutes until golden. Serve.

The chilli we use for the chilli butter in this recipe is in a lot of our Mexican recipes. It is a kind of smoked chilli that comes in a rich sauce and is usually found canned. While very easy to get hold of in America and Latin America, it is slightly harder to come by in Europe (though this is getting better as Mexican food becomes more easily available generally). If you can't find it the closest thing would be to combine a few crushed chilli flakes with a little smoked paprika.

LIME & CHILLI SWEETCORN

SERVES 8–10 AS PART OF A LATIN PARTY

60g (2½oz) salted butter
grated rind of 1 lime
1 chipotle chilli in adobo sauce,
  finely chopped
6–8 corn cobs, husks removed and
  cut into 3 pieces
sea salt flakes

Melt the butter in a small saucepan or a microwave, add the grated lime rind and chopped chilli and mix together well.

Place the corn cob pieces in a large saucepan of boiling water and cook for 3–4 minutes until the corn kernels are just tender.

Remove the corn cob pieces from the water and place them in a hot griddle pan or over a preheated barbecue. Brush the corn with half the chipotle butter and cook, turning every few minutes, until nicely coloured on all sides. Remove from the heat, brush with the remaining butter and season with salt. Serve.

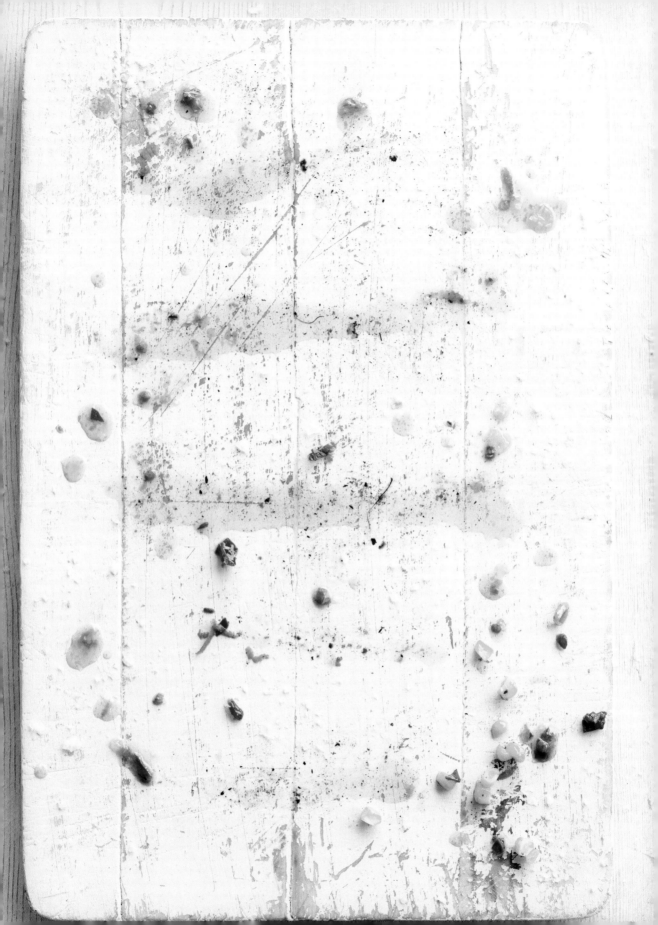

Plantains are one of those things that can seem a bit intimidating if you've never cooked with them before. Although they look like big versions of normal bananas, they do need to be cooked before you can eat them. You can cook with both the green and yellow plantains, though for this recipe you will need the ripe yellow ones (but not the ones that are so ripe they are almost black). If you can't find plantains you can substitute slightly under-ripe normal bananas. To enjoy these fritters at their best you need to eat them straight after cooking.

PLANTAIN FRITTERS

**SERVES 8–10 AS PART OF
A LATIN PARTY**

sunflower oil, for deep-frying
3 ripe plantains, peeled and roughly
  chopped
2 red chillies, trimmed and finely
  chopped
1 small white onion, chopped
handful of coriander leaves
grated rind and juice of 1 lime
1 tablespoon peanut butter
pinch of salt
pinch of chilli powder
100g (3½oz) self-raising flour
Pebre (*see* page 176), to serve

Fill a large saucepan or deep-fryer with sunflower oil and heat to 180°C (350°F), or until a cube of bread thrown into the oil browns in 30 seconds.

Put all the remaining ingredients except the flour in a food processor and blend together until smooth and creamy. Add the flour and blend together again until well combined.

Working in batches, carefully drop small spoonfuls of the mixture into the hot oil and cook for 5 minutes until the fritters have puffed up and are golden brown. Remove from the pan with a slotted spoon and drain on kitchen paper. Serve immediately accompanied by Pebre.

Serve these as a starter before Cinnamon-spiced Squash & Butter Bean Stew (*see* page 120), or serve them alongside the stew as an alternative to the Chilli Cornbread (*see* page 178).

To turn these into a main course, serve with Mexican Salad with Avocado, Baby Gem, Spring Onion & Jalapeño (*see* page 162), Pebre (*see* page 176) and Guacamole (*see* page 175).

Guacamole can be used as a dip or as a side condiment to a variety of dishes. The addition of finely diced tomato or fresh red peppers is a nice variation. We like to make guacamole super smooth when serving it for parties as this makes it easier for dipping; we leave it a bit chunkier when making it to be used as a side or condiment for burritos or tacos.

GUACAMOLE

SERVES 4

3 ripe avocados
½ small red chilli, trimmed, deseeded
  and finely diced
2 tablespoons extra virgin olive oil
juice of 1 lime
handful of coriander leaves, chopped
salt and white pepper

Peel and stone the avocados, place them in a mixing bowl or food processor and add the remaining ingredients. Either mash with a fork to a rough-textured purée or mix well in the food processor to a smooth paste, depending on your preferred texture. Season with salt and pepper to taste and serve.

Use ripe hass avocados for guacamole (they are the blacker, thick-skinned knobbly ones).

To stop guacamole from discolouring if you are making it in advance, don't allow any air to make contact with it. Keep it in a bowl and press cling film right over the surface of the guacamole as well as covering the bowl.

Pebre is a Chilean condiment served alongside almost every dish that is eaten at the dinner table in that country. It is similar to Pico de Gallo (see page 22), or Mexican tomato salsa, but it differs in that it is wetter and more vinegary. This makes it a great accompaniment to empanadas and other Latin dishes, and it is good with a dash or two of Tabasco sauce for a little extra kick. If you can't find very ripe tomatoes, just add a pinch of sugar to the mix.

PEBRE

SERVES 4

5 large ripe tomatoes
1 small banana shallot, finely diced
2 garlic cloves, very finely chopped
1 small red chilli, trimmed and
 finely diced
1 bunch of coriander leaves, chopped
100ml (3½fl oz) olive oil
25ml (1fl oz) water
1 tablespoon red wine vinegar or
 lemon juice
2 teaspoons Tabasco sauce (optional)
salt and pepper

Cut the tomatoes in half and remove the cores, then dice the tomato flesh into small chunks. Add to a mixing bowl with the rest of the ingredients and mix together well. Season with salt and pepper to taste and serve.

Beans, beans are good for your heart, the more you eat, the better they... are! A staple of Mexican and Tex-Mex cuisine, this recipe calls for black beans but pinto or red beans can also be used; if you do so, they should be soaked overnight before cooking. Epazote is a Mexican herb often combined with bean dishes because of its anti-flatulent properties. So while this herb isn't essential to this recipe it's recommended if you can find it! These are great served with a side of corn chips.

BLACK BEAN DIP

SERVES 4–6

200g (7oz) dried black beans
1 teaspoon epazote
1 teaspoon salt
1.2 litres (2 pints) water, plus extra
 if necessary
½ teaspoon bicarbonate of soda
1 bunch of coriander leaves, chopped
2 tablespoons soured cream, to garnish
 (optional)

For the sauce
light oil (such as rapeseed, groundnut
 or sunflower)
½ onion, finely diced
1 small red chilli, trimmed and
 finely diced
2 garlic cloves, very finely chopped
2 teaspoons ground coriander
½ teaspoon ground cumin
2 teaspoons paprika
½ teaspoon cayenne pepper
200g (7oz) canned chopped tomatoes
1 tablespoon tomato purée

Put the beans, epazote and salt in a saucepan, cover with the water and bring to a simmer. Add the bicarbonate of soda and continue to simmer over a low heat for 30–40 minutes, stirring occasionally and adding a little more water if necessary to stop the beans sticking to the bottom of the pan, until the beans have begun to break down and become mushy.

Meanwhile for the sauce, heat a splash of oil in a separate saucepan, add the onion, chilli and garlic and sauté for 5 minutes, until the onion has softened. Add the spices and fry for a further few minutes, stirring, then pour over the chopped tomatoes and tomato purée and bring to a simmer. Cook over a low heat, stirring occasionally, for 15–20 minutes until the mixture is creamy in texture and the flavours have melded together.

Once the beans are ready, tip them into the sauce and stir in the chopped coriander. Spoon into a bowl and garnish with soured cream, if you like.

Gluten-free and deliciously moist, cornbread is a staple food of the American South, and can also be found in Latin America and the Caribbean. It goes really well with our Cinnamon-spiced Squash & Butter Bean Stew (see page 120) and our Borlotti Bean Soup with Smoked Tofu & Pico de Gallo (see page 22).

CHILLI CORNBREAD

**SERVES 8–10 AS PART OF
A LATIN PARTY**

butter, for greasing, plus extra for
  spreading on the bread
250g (8oz) quick-cook polenta, plus
  extra for sprinkling
150g (5oz) sweetcorn kernels
½ red chilli, trimmed and finely diced
2 spring onions, trimmed
100g (3½oz) smoked Cheddar cheese
100g (3½oz) gluten-free plain flour
  (or plain flour, for non gluten-free)
45g (2oz) caster sugar
1 bunch of coriander leaves, chopped
pinch of cayenne pepper
1 teaspoon salt
½ teaspoon baking powder
¼ teaspoon bicarbonate of soda
2 eggs
250ml (8fl oz) milk
120g (4oz) soured cream
50ml (2fl oz) sunflower oil

Preheat the oven to 200°C/fan 180°C/Gas Mark 6. Line the bottom of a 30 x 10-cm (12 x 4-inch) loaf tin with baking parchment. Grease the sides with butter and sprinkle over 2–3 tablespoons of polenta.

Place the remaining polenta and all the other solid ingredients in a bowl and mix together thoroughly. Add the eggs, milk, soured cream and sunflower oil and stir together to combine.

Spoon the cornbread mixture into the prepared loaf tin and bake for 45–50 minutes, until lightly golden and the point of a skewer inserted into the centre of the loaf comes out clean. Cool for a few minutes in the tin before turning out onto a wire rack to cool further before serving, smothered with butter.

SIDES

These very simple yeast-free flatbreads make a great accompaniment to curries and are also excellent filled with spicy pickles and salads.

GARLIC ROTIS

MAKES 8 ROTIS

20g (¾oz) butter
3 garlic cloves, finely chopped
½ teaspoon dried chilli flakes
200g (7oz) self-raising flour, plus extra
  for dusting
50g (2oz) wholemeal self-raising flour
80–100ml (3–3½fl oz) water
vegetable oil

Warm the butter in a small saucepan over a low heat, add the garlic and chilli and cook, stirring, for 1 minute until the garlic has begun to release its flavour but has not yet coloured. Tip into a mixing bowl with the flours and gradually stir in the water with a wooden spoon to form a moist (but not sticky) dough. Knead the dough for a few minutes until smooth, cover with a clean damp cloth and leave for 30 minutes to rise until nearly doubled in size.

Divide the risen dough into 8 pieces and form into balls. Dust with a little flour, then roll out on a lightly floured work surface into thin circles about 5mm ($^1/_4$ inch) thick. Wipe a heavy-based frying pan with just enough oil to grease the base, place over a medium heat and cook the rotis one at a time for 2–3 minutes on each side, until puffed up and brown. Serve immediately, or cover with a clean tea towel and reheat in a low oven when needed.

These fries are very popular at Mildreds and are great served with our Mexican Kidney Bean, Jalapeño, Roasted Pepper & Sweetcorn Burgers and a little Vegan Basil Mayonnaise (see pages 141 and 232). While they are straightforward to make they do require deep-frying, so take care as you go.

SWEET POTATO FRIES

SERVES 4–6 AS A SIDE

3 large sweet potatoes, topped and tailed
1 litre (1¾ pints) sunflower oil
sea salt flakes
3 spring onions, finely chopped (optional)

Scrub the sweet potatoes to remove any dirt but do not peel. Slice into sticks about 1.5cm (³/₄ inch) thick.

Fill a large saucepan or deep-fryer with the sunflower oil and heat to 160°C (325°F), or until a cube of bread thrown into the oil browns in 40 seconds. Add the sweet potatoes in batches, being careful not to overcrowd the pot, and fry for 4–6 minutes until just cooked through but not beginning to colour. Remove with a slotted spoon and turn out on to kitchen paper to drain.

Increase the heat of the oil to 180°C (350°F), or until a cube of bread browns in 30 seconds. Fry the sweet potato fries once again for 2–3 minutes until crisp and golden. Sprinkle with sea salt flakes and scatter over a few chopped spring onions, if desired. Serve.

We like to serve these wedges with our Wild Mushroom & Ale Pies (see page 127) and our burgers. While in the restaurant we often serve these deep-fried, yet they are just as delicious, healthier and a lot less fiddle when roasted like this.

ROAST POTATO WEDGES

SERVES 4–6 AS A SIDE

6 –8 waxy potatoes (such as King Edward)
100ml (3½fl oz) Herb Oil (*see* page 238)
1–2 teaspoons sea salt flakes
5 thyme sprigs, leaves picked

Preheat the oven to 200°C/fan 180°C/Gas Mark 6.

Scrub the potatoes, cut them in half and then into wedges about 1.5cm ($^3/_4$ inch) thick. Put them in a large saucepan and cover with water then rinse and drain (this will remove excess starch). Return the potatoes to the pan, cover with water and bring to the boil. Simmer for 30 seconds then drain.

Pour the Herb Oil into a large roasting tin and heat in the oven for a few minutes. Carefully transfer the parboiled potatoes to the roasting tin, scatter over the sea salt flakes and thyme and shuffle them around to ensure the potato wedges are evenly coated in oil. Roast for 30 minutes, turning halfway through cooking, until crispy and golden brown. Serve.

While we've included these deliciously sweet root veg here in our sides section, they also make a fantastic warm salad when mixed with a few balsamic pickled onions, maple roast pecans and baby spinach leaves.

MAPLE-ROASTED
ROOT VEGETABLES

SERVES 6–8 AS A SIDE

500g (1lb) parsnips, peeled and cut into
   quarters lengthways
400g (13oz) carrots, peeled and cut into
   quarters lengthways
400g (13oz) butternut squash or
   pumpkin, peeled and cut into
   bite-sized pieces
350g (11½oz) beetroot, peeled and cut
   into 1-cm (½-inch wedges)
2 tablespoons maple syrup
100ml (3½fl oz) Herb Oil (*see* page 238)

Preheat the oven to 200°C/fan 180°C/Gas Mark 6. Place a roasting tin in the oven to warm (this will prevent the potatoes from sticking while roasting).

Put the vegetables in a large mixing bowl, pour over the maple syrup and Herb Oil and mix together, ensuring that the vegetables are well coated. Remove the roasting tin from the oven, add the vegetables and spread out evenly. Roast for about 25 minutes, or until the vegetables are golden brown and cooked through. Serve.

If you aren't vegan, **honey** also works well as an alternative to maple syrup here.

These veggies are a nice accompaniment to the **Wild Mushroom & Ale Pies** (*see* page 127).

Lovely and colourful, this is a great summer side. We really recommend making the chilli lemon oil in advance by a day or so, to allow the flavours to mellow and blend together well. While this recipe makes quite a bit of oil, it's so great for dressing vegetables, adding to salads or drizzling over bread before toasting that we're sure you'll use it all up. It will keep refrigerated for at least a week in a sealed container.

CHARGRILLED TENDERSTEM BROCCOLI
WITH CHILLI LEMON OIL

SERVES 4–6 AS A SIDE

400g (13oz) Tenderstem broccoli or
  purple sprouting broccoli
sea salt

For the Chilli Lemon Oil
1 red chilli, trimmed and roughly
  chopped
4 garlic cloves, roughly chopped
juice of ½ lemon
pinch of sea salt flakes
300ml (½ pint) light olive oil

For the chilli lemon oil, put all the ingredients in a measuring jug and blend together with a stick blender for 1–2 minutes. Alternatively, chop the chilli and garlic very finely and then combine with the lemon juice, salt and oil.

Bring a large saucepan of salted water to the boil, add the broccoli spears and blanch for 2–3 minutes until cooked but still firm. Drain.

Heat a ridged griddle pan over a high heat, add the broccoli and chargrill for 2–3 minutes, turning halfway through cooking, until nicely charred and cooked through. Remove from the heat, drizzle with 2–3 tablespoons of the chilli lemon oil and sprinkle with a little sea salt. Serve.

We use this couscous as an accompaniment to our Cauliflower & Green Olive Tagine (see page 136) though it is also very good served with Maple-roasted Root Vegetables (see page 188) and Harissa (see page 228) as a light lunch.

APRICOT & PISTACHIO COUSCOUS

SERVES 6–8 AS A SIDE

100g (3½oz) pistachios
250g (8oz) couscous
2 tablespoons olive oil
grated rind and juice of 1 lemon
100g (3½oz) dried apricots, chopped
300ml (½ pint) boiling water
1 small bunch of flat leaf parsley leaves, chopped
salt and pepper

Toast the pistachios in a dry frying pan over a low heat for 3–4 minutes until beginning to colour. Remove from the heat and set aside.

In a mixing bowl, mix the couscous, olive oil, grated lemon rind, lemon juice and chopped apricots together well. Season with salt and pepper. Pour over the boiling water, cover with clingfilm and leave for 10 minutes until the couscous is fluffy.

Put the pistachios in a food processor and pulse them briefly into small pieces. Stir the nuts through the couscous with the chopped parsley and serve.

This is a lovely warming winter side dish. Try making it up several hours in advance of the rest of your meal (or even the day before) and reheating it before serving, to allow the flavours to develop further.

BRAISED RED CABBAGE

SERVES 6–8 AS A SIDE

1kg (2lb) red cabbage, finely shredded
1 red onion, diced
100g (3½oz) sultanas
½ cinnamon stick
2 bay leaves
30ml (1fl oz) balsamic vinegar
12 juniper berries
50g (2oz) muscovado sugar
250ml (8fl oz) water, plus extra
 if necessary
salt and pepper

Put all the ingredients in a saucepan over a medium heat. Bring to the boil then reduce to a simmer. Cover and cook over a low heat for 45 minutes, stirring occasionally, until the cabbage is tender and the flavours have melded together, adding a little extra water if necessary to stop the cabbage from drying out. Serve.

These onion rings are delicious served with our Beetroot, Fennel, Apple & Dill Burgers (see page 142). Gluten-free flour makes the onion batter really light and less oily.

BEER-BATTERED ONION RINGS

SERVES 4–6 AS A SIDE

vegetable oil, for deep-frying
250g (8oz) gluten-free self-raising flour
  (or self-raising flour, for non gluten-free)
pinch of sea salt flakes
500ml (17fl oz) gluten-free golden ale
  (or golden ale, for non gluten-free)
2 large yellow onions, cut into 1-cm
  (½-inch) slices, rings separated

Half-fill a large saucepan or deep-fryer with vegetable oil and heat to 180°C (350°F), or until a cube of bread thrown into the oil browns in 30 seconds.

Put the flour in a bowl with the sea salt flakes and gradually whisk in the ale to form a batter. Add a handful of the onion rings to the batter and coat them generously.

Drop the battered rings carefully into the hot oil and cook for 3–4 minutes, until crisp and lightly golden. Remove from the oil with a slotted spoon and drain on kitchen paper. Repeat with the remaining onion rings. Serve immediately.

These are great served as an appetiser before our Wild Mushroom & Ale Pies (*see* page 127) or a Sunday lunch on a winter's day.

You can spice up the batter with **course ground mixed pepper** for a spicier finish or even **cumin and chilli** for an Indian flavour – in which case you should serve the onion rings with a **mint yogurt dip**.

A really hearty wintery side dish packed full of vegetables, this is wonderful served with baked potatoes and sautéed greens as a main meal, or spooned over toasted buttery sourdough as a light supper. If you're looking to save time you can use canned beans here; just reduce both the water used for cooking and the time the beans simmer for by half.

MOLASSES BAKED BEANS

SERVES 8–10 AS A SIDE

200g (7oz) dried haricot or cannellini beans
3 tablespoons light olive oil or other light cooking oil (such as rapeseed, groundnut or sunflower)
1 red chilli, trimmed and finely chopped
6 garlic cloves, finely sliced
2 white onions, finely diced
1 small fennel bulb, trimmed, cored and finely diced
2 celery sticks, trimmed, peeled and finely diced
2 carrots, peeled and finely diced
½ cinnamon stick
1 teaspoon smoked paprika
6 bay leaves
2 x 400g (13oz) cans chopped tomatoes
100g (3½oz) tomato purée
1 tablespoon dark brown sugar
2 tablespoons molasses or black treacle
500ml (17fl oz) water
salt

Put the beans in a bowl, cover them with water and leave them to soak overnight.

The next day, drain and rinse the beans. Bring a saucepan of salted water to the boil, tip in the beans and cook for 40–60 minutes, until they are tender but still holding their shape.

Meanwhile, preheat the oven to 180°C/fan 160°C/Gas Mark 4.

Heat the oil in a large saucepan over a medium heat, add the chilli, garlic and onions and sauté for 5–8 minutes until the onions are soft and translucent. Add the fennel, celery and carrots and cook for another 8–10 minutes, stirring, until the vegetables are beginning to soften. Add the cinnamon stick, paprika and bay leaves and cook for another minute before adding the tomatoes, tomato purée, sugar, molasses or black treacle and water. Simmer for 20–25 minutes until all the vegetables are tender and the sauce is thickened.

Spoon the beans and sauce into a casserole or ovenproof dish and mix together well. Cover and bake in the oven for 1 hour until the beans are soft and the flavours have melded together. Serve.

Cooked in the classic style, wet polenta is an excellent accompaniment to Italian dishes such as Baby Aubergine & Roast Pepper Caponata (see page 122).

WET POLENTA

SERVES 6–8 AS A SIDE

900ml (1½ pints) vegetable stock
150g (5oz) quick-cook polenta
50g (2oz) vegetarian Parmesan-style
  hard cheese
50g (2oz) mascarpone cheese
salt and pepper

Pour the vegetable stock into a large saucepan, season with salt and pepper and bring to the boil. Add the polenta, whisking continuously to prevent lumps forming, and simmer for 2–3 minutes, until the polenta has thickened and all the stock has been absorbed.

Remove from the heat, stir in the cheeses and season to taste with salt and pepper. Serve.

Coming from the same family as the cape gooseberry, tomatillos originate in Mexico, where they are a part of the staple cuisine. They give this rice a slightly sour taste, which works nicely as a balance to burritos and other Mexican foods.

TOMATILLO RICE

SERVES 6–8 AS A SIDE

light cooking oil (such as rapeseed, groundnut or sunflower)
1 teaspoon ground coriander
200g (7oz) tomatillos, stalks removed and roughly chopped
400g (13oz) basmati rice, washed thoroughly and strained
400ml (14fl oz) boiling water
salt

Heat a splash of oil in a medium-sized saucepan and lightly fry the ground coriander for 30–40 seconds over a low heat. Add the tomatillos and rice and season with salt.

Pour over the water and bring to the boil, then reduce to a simmer and cook, covered, for 8–10 minutes until the rice is fluffy and cooked through. Remove from the heat and leave to sit, covered, for another 2–3 minutes to steam and fluff up further before serving.

We serve this with our Lapsang-scented Mushroom Stroganoff (see page 132). If walnuts aren't to your taste, crushed hazelnuts or pecans can be used in their place.

WALNUT & LEEK PILAF

SERVES 8–10 AS A SIDE

100g (3½oz) walnut pieces
25g (1oz) butter
1 leek, trimmed, cleaned and diced
1 celery stick, trimmed and diced
700g (1½lb) basmati rice, washed
  thoroughly and strained
800ml (1½ pints) boiling water
1 bunch of dill leaves, chopped

Preheat the oven to 180°C/fan 160°C/Gas Mark 4. Arrange the walnut pieces on a baking tray and toast in the oven for 8–10 minutes until just beginning to colour. Remove from the oven and set aside.

In a small saucepan, melt the butter, add the leek and celery and sauté for 5–8 minutes until soft. Add the washed rice and boiling water, cover and simmer over a low heat for 8–10 minutes, until the rice has absorbed all the water and is tender. Take off the heat and allow to cool a little in the pan, then stir in the walnuts and dill. Serve.

This simple pea pilaf adds a flash of colour to curries and is fragrant without being overpowering.

TURMERIC, PEA & CARDAMOM BASMATI

SERVES 6–8 AS A SIDE

vegetable oil
6 cardamom pods, seeds removed
  and lightly crushed
½ cinnamon stick
¼ teaspoon ground turmeric
½ teaspoon salt
300g (10oz) basmati rice, washed
  thoroughly and strained
400ml (14fl oz) boiling water
200g (7oz) peas, defrosted if frozen

Heat a splash of oil in a small saucepan, add the cardamom and cook for 1 minute, stirring. Add the cinnamon, turmeric and salt and fry for a further minute, then add the basmati rice and boiling water. Bring to a gentle simmer and leave to cook, covered, for 8–10 minutes, until the rice is cooked through. Remove from the heat, stir in the peas, cover with a clean tea towel and set aside for 10 minutes to steam and fluff up further.

DESSERTS

This surprisingly light cheesecake can easily be made gluten-free by substituting gluten-free biscuits for the digestives that make up the gingery base. If you're running short on time, a less labour-intensive version of the cake can be made with fresh berries instead – just fold 200g (7oz) raspberries into the cheesecake filling before spooning over the biscuit base.

WHITE CHOCOLATE & RASPBERRY RIPPLE CHEESECAKE

SERVES 8–10

For the raspberry compote
350g (11½oz) raspberries
80g (3oz) caster sugar
1 teaspoon cornflour
2 tablespoons lemon juice

For the base
200g (7oz) gluten-free digestive
  biscuits (or regular digestive biscuits,
  for non gluten-free)
¼ teaspoon ground ginger
20g (¾oz) demerara sugar
pinch of sea salt flakes
1 piece stem ginger (optional)
60g (2½oz) butter, melted

For the filling
750g (1½lb) cream cheese
20g (¾oz) cornflour
½ teaspoon vanilla extract
finely grated rind of ½ lemon
175g (6oz) caster sugar
2 eggs, plus 1 yolk
150g (5oz) soured cream
150g (5oz) white chocolate chips
  or white chocolate broken into
  small pieces

Preheat the oven to 190°C/fan 170°C/Gas Mark 5. Line a 23-cm (9-inch) springform cake tin with baking parchment.

For the compote, heat 200g (7oz) of the raspberries with the caster sugar in a small saucepan and cook for 5–8 minutes over a gentle heat, stirring occasionally, until the sugar has dissolved. Mix the cornflour together with the lemon juice in a bowl, add to the raspberries and cook until the mix has thickened enough to coat the back of a spoon. Take off the heat and mash with a fork or mix with a stick blender until smooth, then pass through a sieve to remove the seeds. Stir the remaining raspberries into the mix and set aside to cool.

For the base, put the dry ingredients in a food processor with the stem ginger and blend until the mixture resembles fine breadcrumbs. Stir in the butter, then tip into the prepared cake tin and press down into an even layer. Bake for 10 minutes until lightly toasted, then remove and set aside to cool. Reduce the heat to 160°C/fan 140°C/Gas Mark 3.

For the filling, beat the cheese, cornflour, vanilla extract and lemon rind together in a stand mixer or in a bowl with a spoon. Add the sugar, eggs and egg yolk, one at a time, beating together briefly between each addition. Fold in the soured cream and chocolate chips.

To assemble, pour one-third of the compote over the base. Spoon over half the filling then add another third of the compote. Add the rest of the filling and spoon over the remaining compote in three parallel lines. Drag a knife through the lines to create a marbled effect. Bake for 1¼ hours until the filling is starting to colour on the edges and is beginning to firm but is still a bit wobbly. Remove from the oven and leave to cool for at least 3 hours in the refrigerator before serving.

This is a twist on the classic, with apples and ginger cutting through the sweetness and adding extra layers of flavour to this much-loved dessert. This pudding works particularly well with gluten-free flour, though you'll get exactly the same results with regular self-raising flour if you don't have any of the gluten-free stuff to hand. If you like a straightforward sticky toffee pudding, simply omit the ginger and apples.

APPLE & GINGER STICKY TOFFEE PUDDING

SERVES 8–12

300g (10oz) dates
300ml (½ pint) boiling water
4 crisp dessert apples such as Cox's,
  peeled and cored
2–3 stem ginger pieces in syrup
60g (2½oz) butter
250g (8oz) dark muscovado sugar
1 teaspoon vanilla extract
5 eggs
300g (10oz) gluten-free self-raising
  flour or regular self-raising flour
1 teaspoon bicarbonate of soda
1 teaspoon baking powder
1 teaspoon ground ginger
whipped cream, to serve (optional)

For the toffee sauce
120g (4oz) butter
300g (10oz) dark muscovado sugar
1 tablespoon vanilla extract
1 tablespoon stem ginger syrup
½ teaspoon lemon juice
400ml (14fl oz) double cream

Preheat the oven to 190°C/fan 170°C/Gas Mark 5 and line a 30 x 22-cm (12 x 9-inch) ovenproof dish with baking parchment. Put the dates in a bowl, cover with the boiling water and leave to soak.

For the toffee sauce, put all the ingredients except the cream into a saucepan and gently simmer for 5 minutes, stirring occasionally, until the sugar has dissolved and the mixture is a deep caramel colour. Stir in the cream and cook for a further minute then take off the heat.

Cover the base of the prepared tin with a thin layer of the sauce. Cut two of the apples into thin rounds and use these to cover the base of the dish. Drizzle over a little more toffee sauce and set aside the remainder (you should have about half left). Roughly chop the remaining apples, tip into a food processor and pulse to small pieces. Remove and set aside. Put the dates and water in the processor with the stem ginger and blend into chunky pieces.

Cream together the butter, sugar and vanilla extract in a bowl until pale and fluffy. Beat in the eggs one at a time until fully incorporated, then fold in the date mixture. In a separate bowl, mix together the flour, bicarbonate of soda, baking powder, ground ginger and apple pieces. Fold the egg and date mixture into the dry mix and pour into the dish. Bake for 35 minutes or until evenly risen and a skewer inserted into the centre comes out clean. Remove from the oven and leave to cool for 5–10 minutes.

Meanwhile, warm the remaining toffee sauce in the microwave or a small saucepan over a low heat. Turn the pudding out and serve with the warmed toffee sauce and whipped cream, if liked.

This show-stopping celebration cake will delight vegans and non-vegans alike. It can be made in stages in advance to cut down on the work, while the ganache can also be omitted if you are after something lighter and simpler.

CHOCOLATE, COCONUT & BANANA MOUSSE CAKE

SERVES 10–12

For the base
300g (10oz) gluten-free digestive biscuits (or regular digestive biscuits, for non gluten-free)
100g (3½oz) good-quality dark chocolate chips or dark chocolate broken into small pieces (about 50% cocoa solids)
80g (3oz) vegan margarine, melted

For the filling
200ml (7fl oz) apple juice
200ml (7fl oz) maple syrup
100g (3½oz) demerara sugar
7g (¼oz) agar-agar flakes
1 x 200g (7oz) creamed coconut block
5 bananas
500g (1lb) firm silken-style tofu

For the ganache
250ml (8fl oz) soy cream
1 tablespoon golden syrup
350g (11½oz) good-quality dark chocolate chips or dark chocolate broken into small pieces (about 50% cocoa solids)

To decorate
handful of lightly toasted coconut flakes

Line a 25-cm (10-inch) springform cake tin with greaseproof paper.

For the base, put the biscuits and dark chocolate pieces in a food processor and blend together until the mixture resembles fine breadcrumbs. Stir the melted margarine into the crumb mixture, then tip into the prepared cake tin and press down into an even layer. Set aside in the refrigerator to chill until needed.

For the filling, heat the apple juice, maple syrup, sugar and agar-agar flakes in a saucepan and bring to the boil. Reduce the heat and simmer for at least 10 minutes, stirring continuously with a whisk, until the agar-agar is fully dissolved.

Warm the creamed coconut in a microwave and add to the food processor with the juice and syrup mixture, 2 of the bananas and the tofu. Blend together well to a purée consistency.

Slice the remaining bananas and place over the biscuit base then pour over the tofu mixture. Refrigerate for at least 4 hours to chill and set, then remove from the tin and place on a wire rack.

For the ganache, heat the soy cream and golden syrup together in a saucepan until just beginning to bubble. Remove from the heat and stir in the chocolate pieces, then blend together with a stick blender for 2–3 minutes until glossy and smooth. Leave to cool for 2–3 minutes, then spoon into the centre of the cake and smooth over the top and sides with a spatula into an even layer. Chill for at least 1 hour to allow the ganache to set. Decorate with toasted coconut flakes before serving.

Surprisingly simple to make but impressive to serve, this dessert is a perfect summer dinner party finale. Having trialled many different versions using agar-agar as a setting agent in the past, this is by far the easiest we've found and gives the best results too.

PANNA COTTA WITH POACHED NECTARINES

SERVES 6

550ml (17½fl oz) double cream
350ml (12fl oz) semi-skimmed milk
125g (4oz) caster sugar
½ vanilla pod, split lengthways and
  seeds scraped
3 tablespoons agar-agar flakes

For the Poached Nectarines
6 nectarines
rind of ½ lemon
80g (3oz) caster sugar
175ml (6fl oz) rosé wine

Preheat the oven to 180°C/fan 160°C/Gas Mark 4. Lightly grease 6 individual ramekins.

For the poached nectarines, cut the nectarines in half along the seams, twist to open and prise out the stones. Place the nectarine halves cut-side down in an ovenproof dish. Add the lemon rind and sugar, pour over the wine and bake in the oven for 15–20 minutes, until the skins of the nectarines are starting to loosen and wrinkle. Remove from the oven, tip into a bowl and cover with clingfilm. Leave to cool, then remove the nectarine skins and cut into thirds. Strain the nectarine juices and reserve for later.

To make the panna cotta, warm all the ingredients together in a pan. Bring to the boil then immediately lower the heat and cook gently, whisking continuously, for 5 minutes until the mixture has thickened and can coat the back of a spoon.

Strain the mix through a fine sieve and pour into the prepared ramekins. Chill in the refrigerator for at least 3 hours.

To serve, run a knife around the inside of the ramekins and turn the panna cotta out on to individual plates. Spoon a little roasted nectarine around each panna cotta and drizzle over a little of the reserved nectarine juices to finish.

This no-bake cake really couldn't be any simpler to make, though the result is a rich vegan dessert that is perfect for a dinner party. It has featured regularly on our menu with various different fruits for so many years that its origins have been lost in the mists of time – apologies to whoever first came up with it but, rest assured, it is an absolute Mildreds classic. While you do need to use a good-quality dark chocolate to make this cake, don't try using one that is too high in cocoa solids as anything more than 55% will cause the mixture to separate.

DARK CHOCOLATE & RASPBERRY TRUFFLE CAKE

SERVES 10–12

750ml (1¼ pints) soy cream, plus extra to serve
1kg (2lb) good-quality dark chocolate chips or dark chocolate broken into small pieces (about 50% cocoa solids)
500g (1lb) raspberries, plus an extra handful to decorate
cocoa powder, to dust

Line the base and sides of a 23-cm (9-inch) springform cake tin with baking parchment.

Pour the soy cream into a large saucepan. Bring to the boil, then remove from the heat and stir in the chocolate pieces with a spoon. Whisk together briskly by hand for 5 minutes or blend with a stick blender for 3–4 minutes until glossy and smooth, then carefully fold in the raspberries. Spoon the mixture into the prepared tin and smooth the surface (a careful bang on the counter will help do this), then refrigerate for at least 3 hours until firm and cool.

When ready to serve, open the tin and remove the parchment from the sides. Take a large serving plate and place it over the cake, then turn the cake and plate over and remove the bottom layer of parchment. Decorate the cake with a dusting of cocoa and a few more raspberries. Serve, cut into slices, with soy cream.

A favourite at Mildreds ever since it was introduced by Daniel Strutt, this dessert has a creamy texture that marries well with the tartness of the passion fruit. If you can source passion fruit purée it will cut down on the work here. Decorate with homemade ginger snaps, or omit these for a gluten-free option.

PASSION FRUIT CRÈME CARAMEL
WITH GINGER SNAPS

SERVES 8

350g (11½oz) caster sugar
500ml (17fl oz) double cream
150ml (¼ pint) semi-skimmed milk
6 large eggs
seeds of 1 passion fruit, to decorate

For the passion fruit juice
either use 200ml (7fl oz) of passion
  fruit purée (available in good off-
  licences and catering supply shops)
  or 8–10 passion fruit (making 250ml/
  8fl oz of seeds and flesh)
30g (1oz) caster sugar
100ml (3½fl oz) water

For the Ginger Snaps
50g (2oz) butter
50g (2oz) golden syrup
50g (2oz) muscovado sugar
50g (2oz) plain flour
½ teaspoon ground ginger

Preheat the oven to 190°C/fan 170°C/Gas Mark 5. Line a baking tray with baking parchment. For the passion fruit juice, scoop out the seeds and flesh from the passion fruit and add to a saucepan. Add the sugar and water and bring to the boil. Lower the heat and simmer for 3–5 minutes, until the sugar has dissolved. Strain and set aside.

For the ginger snaps, melt the butter, syrup and sugar in a saucepan until the sugar is dissolved. Remove from the heat and whisk in the flour and ginger. Place teaspoonfuls of the mixture on to the prepared baking tray 10cm (4 inches) apart and bake for 10 minutes or until they are golden brown with bubbles on the surface. Remove from the oven and leave to cool on the tray, then store in an airtight container, separated by baking parchment to prevent sticking, until needed. Reduce the heat to 150°C/fan 130°C/Gas Mark 2.

Arrange 8 x 200-ml (7-fl oz) dariole moulds or standard ramekins on a deep oven tray. Put 150g (5oz) of the sugar in a small saucepan and cover with water. Leave the sugar on a high heat without stirring until it starts to catch, then swirl it in the pan, turn down the heat and cook until a dark caramel colour. Spoon 2 tablespoons of the caramel over the bases of the moulds, moving fast as the caramel will keep cooking.

In a mixing bowl, whisk together the remaining sugar with the passion fruit juice, cream, milk and eggs until combined. Strain into a measuring jug, then use to fill the moulds. Half-fill the tray with water and bake the caramels in the middle of the oven for 1 hour, or until risen slightly. Remove from the tray and refrigerate for at least 2 hours or until fully set. To serve, run a small knife around the edge of each caramel and turn on to plates. Decorate with passion fruit seeds.

This delicious gluten-free cake, with its beautiful jewelled topping of pomegranates, rose petals and pistachios, takes inspiration from two places – a Persian walnut cake in Claudia Rodin's Jewish Food as well as the classic River Café lemon polenta cake. It is filled with the Middle Eastern flavours of the former and has all the moistness of the latter, though only about half the fat.

PERSIAN SPICED ALMOND, PISTACHIO & POLENTA CAKE WITH ROSE PETAL & POMEGRANATE SYRUP

SERVES 8–10

150g (5oz) shelled pistachios, plus a handful to decorate
200g (7oz) butter
400g (13oz) caster sugar
grated rind of 4 lemons, plus juice of 2
5 eggs, separated
250g (8oz) ground almonds
200g (7oz) polenta
1 teaspoon baking powder
pinch of salt

For the Rose Petal and Pomegranate Syrup
juice of 3 lemons
100ml (3½fl oz) water
1 tablespoon rosewater
200g (7oz) caster sugar
2 cardamom pods
2 star anise
½ cinnamon stick
1 tablespoon rose petals
handful of shelled pistachios, roughly chopped
1 pomegranate, seeds removed

Preheat the oven to 190°C/fan 170°C/Gas Mark 5. Line a 23-cm (9-inch) cake tin with baking parchment. Cut out a piece of parchment to match the size of the tin and set aside.

Tip the pistachios into a food processor and blend them to a fine powder. Set aside.

Cream the butter, sugar and lemon juice together in a stand mixer or in a bowl with a spoon until pale and fluffy. Beat in the egg yolks a couple at a time. Fold in the ground almonds, ground pistachios, polenta, grated lemon rind, baking powder and salt, being careful not to over-mix.

Whisk the egg whites until fairly stiff and fold into the mix. Pour the cake mix into the prepared tin and cover with the loose piece of parchment. Bake on the lower shelf of the oven for 1¼ hours, remove the parchment and bake for a further 15 minutes or until the cake is evenly risen and springs back when lightly pressed with a finger.

To make the syrup, put the lemon juice, water, rosewater, sugar and spices in a pan and cook over a medium heat for 3–5 minutes, until the sugar has dissolved and the syrup has thickened and reduced slightly. Strain to remove the spices, add the rose petals and pistachios and set aside to cool. Once cool, stir in the pomegranate seeds.

Prick the cake all over with a toothpick and cover with the syrup. Scatter over a few whole pistachios to decorate. Serve.

If you're hunting for a posh-looking pudding to add to your repertoire that requires very little time and even less skill to put together, then look no further. This is a lovely summer dessert full of bright colours and fresh flavours.

MANGO FOOL WITH MINT SUGAR & BLACK SESAME BRITTLE

SERVES 6–8

150ml (¼ pint) water
80g (3oz) caster sugar
juice of 1 lime
2 small ripe honey mangoes or 1 large
  ripe mango, peeled and chopped,
  plus extra cubes to decorate
1 teaspoon cornflour
350ml (12oz) double cream

For the Black Sesame Brittle
2 tablespoons black sesame seeds
200g (7oz) caster sugar

For the Mint Sugar
5 mint leaves
50g (2oz) demerara sugar
grated rind of ½ lime

Put the water, sugar and lime juice in a saucepan and bring to the boil. Lower the heat to a simmer, add the mango and cook for 2–3 minutes until the mango begins to break down. Mix the cornflour with a little water to form a smooth paste and add to the saucepan. Simmer gently for 3 minutes until the mixture is thick enough to coat the back of a spoon, then remove from the heat and blend with a stick blender to a smooth purée. Leave to cool.

Whip the cream in a bowl to soft peaks. Carefully fold in two-thirds of the mango purée. Refrigerate the fool and remaining mango purée until ready to assemble.

For the black sesame brittle, line a baking tray with baking parchment. Gently toast the sesame seeds in a saucepan over a low heat for 1–2 minutes until fragrant. Remove the seeds from the pan and set aside. Add the sugar to the pan and heat gently, without stirring, until melted and light caramel in colour. Add the sesame seeds and cook for another minute then pour the mixture on to the prepared baking tray. Spread as thinly as possible. Leave to cool, then snap into shards about 5–10cm (2–4 inches) in length.

To make the mint sugar, blend the ingredients together with a hand-held blender using the mixer attachment, or in a spice grinder.

To assemble the fools, coat the rims of 6–8 martini or margarita glasses with the mint sugar. Spoon a layer of fool into the bottom of each glass, top with a layer of mango purée and finish with another layer of fool. Sprinkle over the cubes of mango and decorate with the sesame brittle shards. Serve.

This is our vegan take on American pecan pie. We've reduced the sweetness of the original and added more nuts, while the traditional creamy filling has been transformed through the addition of silken tofu. To give it a boozy, rich flavour, add some bourbon to the caramel after taking it off the heat.

MAPLE PECAN PIE WITH VEGAN SWEET PASTRY

SERVES 8–10

100ml (3½fl oz) maple syrup
250g (8oz) light brown sugar
1 teaspoon vanilla extract
grated rind of ½ small orange and juice
  of 1 orange
100g (3½oz) vegan margarine
½ teaspoon salt
5 tablespoons bourbon whiskey
  (optional)
255g (8oz) siken tofu
30g (1oz) cornflour
pinch of ground cinnamon
½ vanilla pod, split lengthways and
  seeds scraped
100ml (3½fl oz) unsweetened soy milk
225g (7½oz) pecans, plus 25 halves
  for topping
cream or ice cream, to serve (optional)

For the Vegan Sweet Pastry
250g (8oz) plain flour, plus extra
  for dusting
40g (1½oz) light brown sugar
pinch of salt
pinch of ground cinnamon
grated rind and juice of 1 orange
125g (4oz) vegan margarine, chilled
20ml (¾fl oz) iced water
2 teaspoons apple cider vinegar

Preheat the oven to 170°C/fan 150°C/Gas Mark 4. Line a 23-cm (9-inch) loose-bottomed tart tin with baking parchment. Cut out another piece of parchment to match the size of the tin and set aside.

For the pastry, place the flour, sugar, salt, cinnamon and grated orange rind in a bowl, add the margarine and rub in with the fingertips until the mixture resembles fine breadcrumbs. Add the water, vinegar and orange juice and bring together to form a dough. Roll into a ball, wrap in clingfilm and chill in the refrigerator for at least 30 minutes.

Roll out the pastry on a lightly floured surface to a thickness of 5mm ($^1/_4$ inch). Use it to line the tart tin. Cover the pastry with the piece of baking parchment and fill with ceramic baking beans. Bake the pastry for 20–25 minutes, removing the beans for the final 5 minutes of cooking, until lightly golden and cooked through.

Put the syrup, sugar, vanilla, orange rind juice in a saucepan. Bring to the boil, lower the heat and simmer, stirring frequently, for about 3 minutes until the mix has reduced to a thick light caramel. Remove from the heat and stir in the margarine, salt and bourbon, if using.

Blend together the tofu, cornflour, cinnamon and vanilla seeds in a food processor until smooth. Continue to blend, gradually adding the soy milk, until the mixture has the consistency of double cream. Add the caramel and blend, then add the pecans and pulse for a few seconds until the pecans are reduced to roughly 1.5-cm ($^3/_4$-inch) pieces.

Pour the filling into the case and spread evenly. Top with the pecan halves and bake in the centre of the oven for 1–1$^1/_4$ hours, until the filling is soft but set, the top is slightly raised and a crust has formed. Cool slightly then serve warm with cream or ice cream, if you like.

We have tried tons of different brownie recipes over the years, vegan and otherwise, but this simple version is one of the best we've found. If you don't tell, no-one will know these brownies are vegan; they are rich, squishy and chocolatey and everything a brownie should be. You don't have to bother serving the brownies with the chocolate sauce, though it does give them a little something extra. One note of caution; don't be sloppy when weighing the dry ingredients, as ten grammes either way will make a difference to the bake.

PEANUT BUTTER BROWNIES
WITH HOT CHOCOLATE SAUCE

SERVES 8–12

320g (11oz) wheat-free flour
240g (8oz) dark muscovado sugar
240g (8oz) light muscovado sugar
120g (4oz) cocoa powder
1 teaspoon baking powder
pinch of salt
150g (5oz) good-quality chunky
  peanut butter
225ml (7½fl oz) water
225ml (7½fl oz) vegetable oil
2 tablespoons good-quality
  vanilla extract
60g (2½oz) good-quality dark
  chocolate chips or dark chocolate
  broken into small pieces (about 50%
  cocoa solids)
vanilla ice cream, to serve

For the Hot Chocolate Sauce
250ml (8fl oz) soy cream
1 tablespoon golden syrup
120g (4oz) good-quality dark chocolate
  chips or dark chocolate broken into
  small pieces (about 50% cocoa solids)
30g (1oz) dark muscovado sugar
70g (3oz) cocoa powder
250ml (8fl oz) water, plus extra
  if necessary

Preheat the oven to 170°C/fan 150°C/Gas Mark 4. Line a 20 x 30-cm (8 x 12-inch) baking tin with baking parchment.

Put the flour, sugars, cocoa powder, baking powder and salt in a bowl and mix together thoroughly to remove any lumps. Add a tablespoon of the peanut butter, the water, oil, vanilla extract and chocolate and beat with a whisk for 2–3 minutes to combine. The mix should be the texture of whipped cream; if it looks too thick, add a little more water. Pour the mix into the prepared tin and even out.

Put the remaining peanut butter in a piping bag and use to pipe lines over the brownie mix, making sure that you reach the edges. Drag a knife through the top layer of the mix in the opposite direction to the lines to create a marbled effect. Bake for 45–50 minutes (or until semi-firm in the centre). Set aside to cool.

For the sauce, heat the cream and syrup in a saucepan over a medium heat until they begin to boil, then remove from the heat and stir in the chocolate. Whisk the sugar, cocoa and water together in a bowl and pour into the chocolate mixture. Whisk well and return to the heat to warm through. Whisk briskly together for 5 minutes or blend with a stick blender for 3 minutes until glossy and smooth.

Cut the brownies into squares with a sharp knife and serve with the warm chocolate sauce and vanilla ice cream, if liked.

DIPS, SAUCES & DRESSINGS

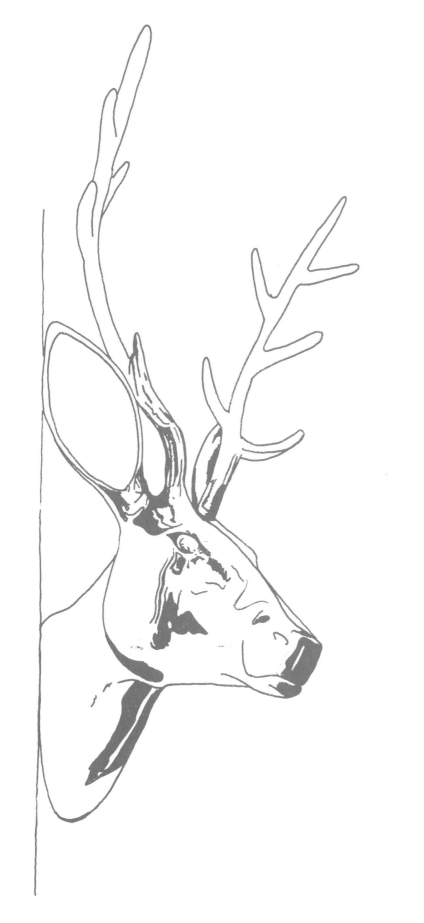

While there are a lot of decent store-bought varieties of harissa available, if you haven't made it from scratch before give this a go as it is one of those things that really benefits from being homemade. As with a lot of spiced sauces, the flavours will deepen and develop, so it's a good thing to make a day or two in advance. You might find this harissa quite mild – if you really like heat, just add a couple more chillies.

HARISSA

MAKES APPROXIMATELY 300ML (½ PINT)

60ml (2fl oz) light olive oil
3 red peppers
2 red chillies, trimmed
1½ tablespoons cumin seeds
1½ tablespoons smoked paprika
2 teaspoons tomato purée
2 garlic cloves, peeled
handful of coriander leaves

Preheat the oven to 240°C/fan 220°C/Gas Mark 9.

Drizzle a third of the olive oil on to the base of a roasting tin. Add the peppers and chillies and mix together thoroughly. Roast for 15 minutes, until the peppers and chillies have puffed up and are starting to split open. Transfer them to a bowl, cover with clingfilm and set aside to cool for 15 minutes. Once cool enough to handle, tear the peppers and chillies open, removing the cores and seeds. Peel off the skins and set the flesh aside.

Toast the cumin seeds in a dry frying pan over a medium heat for about a minute until fragrant. Using a pestle and mortar, grind the toasted cumin together with the smoked paprika.

Combine all the ingredients in a measuring jug and blend with a stick blender until smooth. For a really smooth harissa, pass the mixture through a sieve or chinois.

This spicy paste packed with Middle-Eastern flavours is similar to the commonly found red pepper harissa, although it is considerably less spicy, with the green vegetables and mint giving it a much fresher finish. It can be used as a dressing or as an accompaniment to dishes such as tagine.

GREEN HARISSA

MAKES APPROXIMATELY 400ML (14FL OZ)

6 green chillies, trimmed
1 teaspoon cumin seeds
1 teaspoon fennel seeds
1 teaspoon sumac
2 teaspoons chilli flakes
400ml (14fl oz) light olive or
  rapeseed oil
handful each of mint, flat leaf parsley
  and coriander leaves
grated rind and juice of 2 lemons
300g (10oz) peas, defrosted if frozen
4 spring onions, trimmed
6 garlic cloves, peeled

Preheat the oven to 240°C/fan 220°C/Gas Mark 9.

Arrange the chillies on a baking tray and roast for 15 minutes, until they have puffed up and are starting to split open. Transfer them to a bowl, cover with clingfilm and set aside to cool for 15 minutes. Once cool enough to handle, tear the chillies open, removing the cores and seeds. Peel off the skins and set the chilli flesh aside.

Toast the cumin and fennel seeds in a dry frying pan over a medium heat for about a minute until fragrant. Using a pestle and mortar, grind the toasted spices together with the sumac and chilli flakes.

Combine all the ingredients in a measuring jug and blend with a stick blender until smooth. For a really smooth harissa, pass the mixture through a sieve or chinois.

A lot of the success of this Mediterranean dip depends on the quality of the haricot beans used. We use a Spanish variety that are softer than usual and work particularly well here; quite often the type that come in jars are slightly better than the ones in tins.

POTATO & WHITE BEAN DIP

SERVES 4–6

370g (12oz) waxy potatoes, peeled and halved
4 garlic cloves
40g (1½oz) ground almonds
400g (13oz) canned or jarred haricot beans, drained and rinsed
100ml (3½fl oz) extra virgin olive oil, plus extra to garnish
pinch of white pepper
juice of 1 lemon
1 tablespoon cider vinegar
pinch of sweet paprika, to garnish

Put the halved potatoes in a large saucepan, cover with water and bring to the boil. Reduce the heat and simmer for 15–20 minutes until cooked through.

Drain the cooked potatoes and tip into a food processor along with the rest of the ingredients. Blend until smooth. Serve garnished with a drizzle of olive oil and a sprinkling of paprika and accompanied by warm pitta bread.

Sambal is a hot, spicy condiment served alongside various South East Asian and Indian dishes. With the addition of fresh herbs and spices, this version has a sweet yet powerful kick that shouldn't overload your mouth with heat, though it's worth adding the raw chilli at the end gradually to achieve a spice level that you are comfortable with.

TOMATO & COCONUT SAMBAL

MAKES APPROXIMATELY 700ML (1¼ PINTS)

light cooking oil (such as rapeseed, groundnut or sunflower)
12 fresh or frozen curry leaves
2 small onions, diced
1 teaspoon chilli powder
1 teaspoon salt
400g (13oz) can chopped tomatoes
3 tablespoons tomato purée
2 tablespoons caster sugar
2 green chillies, trimmed and finely chopped
handful of coriander leaves, chopped
20g (¾oz) fresh root ginger, peeled and chopped
30g (1oz) desiccated coconut

Heat a splash of oil in a small saucepan, add the curry leaves and fry briefly for 10–15 seconds, being careful not to burn them. Add the onions and cook, stirring, for 5 minutes until they have started to soften. Add the chilli powder and cook for a few minutes more, then add the salt, chopped tomatoes, tomato purée and sugar and simmer over a low heat for 15–20 minutes until the sambal has thickened and reduced and the flavours have melded together.

Remove from the heat and blend the sauce with a stick blender or in a food processor to a smooth consistency. Set aside and leave to cool.

Once cool, stir the chillies, coriander leaves, ginger and desiccated coconut through the sambal and mix together thoroughly. Transfer to a suitable container and refrigerate for up to a week.

This is our classic vegan mayo that accompanies all our burgers and fries, although it is also good mixed into a potato salad or thinned a little and used as a regular salad dressing. It will keep for up to two weeks in the refrigerator.

VEGAN BASIL MAYONNAISE

MAKES APPROXIMATELY 500ML (17FL OZ)

1 small bunch of basil leaves
2 garlic cloves
1 tablespoon Dijon mustard
150ml (¼ pint) unsweetened soy milk
300ml (½ pint) light oil (such as
  rapeseed, vegetable or sunflower)
salt and pepper

Put all the ingredients in a large measuring jug and season with salt and pepper. Blend with a stick blender until all the oil is incorporated. If the mayo looks too thick, add a little more soy milk or water. Transfer to a suitable container and refrigerate until needed.

You can substitute other herbs for the basil in this recipe; for example **chervil** or **tarragon** or a **mixture of green herbs**.

If you don't eat soy products, use **almond milk** instead of soy milk.

This is a mild aioli that pairs wonderfully with grilled veggies, warm salads, roast potato wedges and our Artichoke Crostini (see page 52). It will keep in the refrigerator for up to a week.

ROAST GARLIC & LEMON AIOLI

MAKES APPROXIMATELY 400ML (14FL OZ)

7 garlic cloves, peeled
300ml (½ pint) light olive oil, plus extra for drizzling
2 egg yolks
juice of ½ lemon
1 tablespoon Dijon mustard
½ teaspoon white pepper
50ml (2fl oz) boiling water
salt

Preheat the oven to 180°C/fan 160°C/Gas Mark 4.

Place the garlic cloves in the centre of a small of tray of aluminium foil, drizzle with a little oil and seal to form a parcel. Roast in the oven for 15 minutes, or until the garlic is just beginning to brown. Set aside to cool.

Place the cooled garlic cloves, egg yolks, lemon juice, mustard and white pepper in a food processor and blend together until puréed. With the motor running, pour over the oil in a thin, steady stream, gradually adding the boiling water as you go to prevent the mix from splitting. Season to taste with salt. Transfer to a suitable container and refrigerate until needed.

Truffle oil varies so hugely in strength that we haven't put an exact quantity here; instead we urge you to add a little, taste, and adjust the amount until you are satisfied it's strong enough. Remember the flavour will develop and deepen, so it's better to err on the side of caution than end up with something that's too overpowering.

TRUFFLE MAYONNAISE

MAKES APPROXIMATELY 300ML (½ PINT)

50ml (2fl oz) light oil (such as rapeseed, groundnut or sunflower), plus extra if necessary
100ml (3½fl oz) light olive oil
truffle oil, to taste
100ml (3½fl oz) soy cream
juice of ½ lemon
1 teaspoon Dijon mustard
salt and pepper

Mix the sunflower and olive oils together in a measuring jug. Stir in the truffle oil a few drops at a time, tasting and continuing to add more until the oil mix has a light truffle flavour.

Place the soy cream, lemon juice and mustard in a food processor, season to taste with salt and pepper and blend together. With the motor running, pour over the oil in a thin, steady stream until you get a thick, creamy mayonnaise, adding a little extra sunflower oil if needed. Transfer to a suitable container and refrigerate until needed (the mayonnaise will keep for a week or two).

We serve this rich gravy with our Roasted Portobello Mushroom, Pecan & Chestnut Wellington (see page 125).

PORT GRAVY

MAKES APPROXIMATELY 1.2 LITRES (2 PINTS)

2 tablespoons olive oil
½ small white onion, roughly chopped
½ carrot, roughly chopped
1 celery stick, trimmed and roughly chopped
2 garlic cloves
1 thyme sprig
1 rosemary sprig
1 litre (1¾ pints) water
1 teaspoon vegetable bouillon powder
500ml (17fl oz) vegetarian port
2 tablespoons gluten-free plain flour (or plain flour for non gluten-free)
1½ tablespoons tomato purée
1½ tablespoons tamari (gluten-free soy sauce)

Heat the oil in a large saucepan over a medium–high heat. Add the onion, carrot, celery, garlic and herbs to the pan and fry for 5 minutes or so, stirring, until the vegetables soften and start to colour. Add the water and bouillon powder and bring to the boil. Reduce the heat to a simmer and cook gently for 20 minutes. Remove the stock from the heat and strain, discarding the vegetables and herbs.

Pour the port into another large saucepan and simmer until reduced to just a couple of tablespoons of liquid. Add the flour and whisk together to form a roux. Stir in the tomato purée and tamari.

Whisking continuously to prevent lumps, gradually add the stock. Simmer gently until the gravy is thickened and glossy.

We've served this relish with our veggie burgers at Mildreds for more than 15 years. It's a recipe that has been handed down to us by former head chef Gillian Snowball. It adds a delicious sweet piquancy to burgers and sandwiches, or when served with cheese and biscuits. As it is a preserve, you can store it in sterilized jars for a couple of weeks.

CARROT RELISH

**MAKES APPROXIMATELY
3 X 400-ML (14-FL OZ) JARS**

550g (1¼lb) grated carrot
700g (1½lb) bramley cooking apples,
  peeled, cored and quartered
300g (10oz) dark muscovado sugar
250ml (8fl oz) cider vinegar
5 tablespoons tomato purée
250g (8oz) sultanas
250ml (8fl oz) apple juice

Place all the ingredients in a large saucepan. Cover and bring to a simmer, then lower the heat and cook gently, stirring occasionally, for 25–30 minutes, until the relish has thickened and reduced.

Remove from the heat and blend well in a food processor or with a stick blender to form a smooth paste. Decant into sterilized jars and keep for up to two weeks in the refrigerator.

It's great to have a jar of this to hand; it adds loads of flavour to roast vegetables, and making a batch up to use whenever you need it will save chopping herbs and garlic later. It should keep for well over a week in the refrigerator.

HERB OIL

MAKES APPROXIMATELY
500ML (17FL OZ)

500ml light oil (such as rapeseed,
 groundnut or sunflower)
4 garlic cloves
3 rosemary sprigs
3 thyme sprigs
salt

Put the oil, garlic, rosemary and thyme in a measuring jug, season with salt and blend with a stick blender until smooth. Alternatively, chop the garlic, rosemary and thyme leaves, put in a jar or bottle with a screw-top lid along with the oil and salt and shake together until well combined.

Purple basil, also confusingly called red basil, has leaves that are a wonderful dark purple colour, though when they are blended up like this the colour changes to a lovely dark pink. If you can't find purple basil, just swap in regular green basil – the flavour will be the same, if not the colour.

PURPLE BASIL OIL

MAKES APPROXIMATELY
200ML (7FL OZ)

1 large bunch of purple basil leaves
grated rind and juice of 1 lemon
200ml (7fl oz) light olive oil
salt and pepper

Place all the ingredients in a measuring jug, season with salt and pepper and blend with a stick blender until smooth.

This Vegetarian Caesar Dressing tastes just as good as the original, which many people wrongly assume to be vegetarian (it isn't as it contains anchovies). Henderson's Relish works nicely to give this dressing the tang it needs – it can be tricky to find outside the north of England, though, in which case look for vegetarian Worcestershire sauce in your local health food shop instead.

**MAKES APPROXIMATELY
400ML (14FL OZ)**

250ml (8fl oz) soy cream
1 garlic clove
juice of 1 lemon
1 teaspoon Henderson's Relish or
  vegetarian Worcestershire sauce
½ teaspoon Tabasco sauce
pinch of white pepper
pinch of cayenne pepper
pinch of salt
1 teaspoon Dijon mustard
50g (2oz) vegetarian Parmesan-style
  hard cheese, grated
150ml (¼ pint) light olive or
  rapeseed oil

VEGETARIAN CAESAR DRESSING

Put all the ingredients except the oil in a food processor along with a splash of water and blend until smooth. With the motor running, pour over the oil in a steady stream until the dressing is thick and shiny, adding a little extra splash of water if it thickens too much.

This zesty and slightly spicy dressing is great for Latin salads. Chipotle chillies are mild, smokey chillies usually sold canned.

**MAKES APPROXIMATELY
350ML (12FL OZ)**

2 chipotle chilli peppers
grated rind and juice of 1 lime
juice of 1 lemon
250ml (8fl oz) olive or rapeseed oil
1 teaspoon tomato purée
2 teaspoons icing sugar

CHIPOTLE LIME DRESSING

Place all the ingredients in a measuring jug and blend with a stick blender until smooth. Alternatively, chop the chillies, put in a jar or bottle with a screw-top lid along with all the other ingredients and shake together until well combined.

A very simple dressing to make with simple fresh flavours, this pairs well with lots of salads and is really tasty tossed over fresh green vegetables.

MAKES APPROXIMATELY 350ML (12FL OZ)

handful of mint leaves
1 garlic clove
grated rind of 1½ lemons and juice of 3 lemons
150ml (¼ pint) light olive oil
salt and pepper
1 teaspoon Dijon mustard
1 teaspoon icing sugar

LEMON MINT DRESSING

Place all the ingredients in a small jug and blend with a stick blender until smooth. Alternatively, chop the mint and garlic, put in a jar or bottle with a screw-top lid along with all the other ingredients and shake together until well combined.

A tangy Asian dressing that is perfect for noodle salads and salads which feature Asian vegetables. It can also be used as a stir-fry sauce.

MAKES APPROXIMATELY 200ML (7FL OZ)

1 red chilli, trimmed
2 garlic cloves
handful of coriander leaves
5g (¼oz) fresh root ginger, peeled
grated rind and juice of 1 lime
1 teaspoon tamarind paste
1 tablespoon sesame seeds, lightly toasted
50ml (2fl oz) gluten-free sweet chilli sauce
150ml (¼ pint) sesame oil
2 tablespoons tamari (gluten-free soy sauce)

SESAME CHILLI DRESSING

Place all the ingredients in a measuring jug and blend with a stick blender until smooth. Alternatively, chop the chilli, garlic, coriander and ginger, put in a jar or bottle with a screw-top lid along with all the other ingredients and shake together until well combined.

**MAKES APPROXIMATELY
350ML (12FL OZ)**

2 garlic cloves
3 thyme sprigs, leaves picked
2 rosemary sprigs, leaves picked
juice of 2 oranges plus grated rind of 1
50ml (2fl oz) maple syrup
100ml (3½fl oz) olive oil
½ teaspoon Dijon mustard
½ teaspoon wholegrain mustard

Another simple dressing to make, this goes very well with salad but is also delicious served with warm roast vegetables.

ORANGE MAPLE DRESSING

Place all the ingredients in a measuring jug and blend with a stick blender until smooth. Alternatively, chop the garlic, thyme and rosemary, put in a jar or bottle with a screw-top lid along with all the other ingredients and shake together until well combined.

**MAKES APPROXIMATELY
150ML (¼ PINT)**

75ml (3fl oz) tahini paste
juice of 1 lemon
¼ teaspoon sumac
2 tablespoons maple syrup

This rich, nutty, Middle Eastern dressing is a great addition to salads and vegetable dishes.

TAHINI DRESSING

Put the tahini paste, lemon juice, sumac and maple syrup in a food processor and season with salt and pepper. Blend together, gradually adding water as you go, until the dressing has the consistency of double cream. (You can do this by hand with a whisk if you like, but you may get a few lumps.) Taste and adjust the seasoning as necessary.

GLUTEN-FREE MENU IDEAS

MENU ONE

MENU TWO

MENU THREE

MENU ONE

PRIMAVERA SALAD WITH
HOMEMADE LEMON RICOTTA
(*SEE* PAGE 102)

LAPSANG-SCENTED
MUSHROOM STROGANOFF
(*SEE* PAGE 132)

PANNA COTTA WITH
POACHED NECTARINES
(*SEE* PAGE 209)

MENU TWO

SPRING VEGETABLE PAKORA WITH
MANGO YOGURT DIP
(*SEE* PAGE 49)

SRI LANKAN SWEET POTATO
& CASHEW NUT CURRY
(*SEE* PAGE 115)

PERSIAN SPICED ALMOND,
PISTACHIO & POLENTA CAKE
WITH ROSE PETAL &
POMEGRANATE SYRUP
(*SEE* PAGE 216)

MENU THREE

MANGO SUMMER ROLLS
WITH SPICY PEANUT SAUCE
(*SEE* PAGE 37)

PEA, CARROT, PEPPER
& TOFU LAKSA
(*SEE* PAGE 108)

MANGO FOOL WITH MINT
SUGAR & BLACK
SESAME BRITTLE
(*SEE* PAGE 218)

VEGAN MENU IDEAS

MENU ONE

MENU TWO

MENU THREE

MENU ONE	MENU TWO	MENU THREE
PUY LENTIL SALAD WITH ROASTED VEGETABLES (*SEE* PAGE 87)	ARTICHOKE CROSTINI WITH VEGAN BASIL MAYONNAISE (*SEE* PAGES 52 & 232)	STUFFED BABY AUBERGINES WITH TAHINI DRESSING (*SEE* PAGES 67 & 243)
ROASTED PORTOBELLO MUSHROOM, PECAN & CHESTNUT WELLINGTON (*SEE* PAGE 125)	BLACK BEAN CHILLI FILLED BABY PUMPKINS WITH TOASTED COCONUT RICE (*SEE* PAGE 130)	CAULIFLOWER & GREEN OLIVE TAGINE (*SEE* PAGE 136)
MAPLE-ROASTED ROOT VEGETABLES (*SEE* PAGE 188)	MAPLE PECAN PIE WITH VEGAN SWEET PASTRY (*SEE* PAGE 221)	APRICOT & PISTACHIO COUSCOUS (*SEE* PAGE 192)
BRAISED RED CABBAGE (*SEE* PAGE 193)		PEANUT BUTTER BROWNIES WITH HOT CHOCOLATE SAUCE (*SEE* PAGE 223)
DARK CHOCOLATE & RASPBERRY TRUFFLE CAKE (*SEE* PAGE 212)		

SUPPLIERS

Although supermarkets stock a wider range of speciality products these days, you can still find yourself running around to two or three different supermarkets trying to source all the ingredients you're looking for to execute that special dinner. I always put some trust into my local Italian deli, Middle Eastern grocer or Asian/Oriental supermarket so check these out if you're lucky enough to have one nearby.

If you find your local shops don't accommodate for speciality items the list of the following local and online suppliers will hopefully save you some time when looking around for the right ingredients.

Brindisa

One of our long-standing suppliers of piquillo peppers, butterbeans, Spanish paprika and chickpeas (or garbanzos, as they are advertised on their website). They have some of the best quality cooked beans and pulses around, all available online as well as from their stores in London's Borough and Brixton markets.
www.brindisa.com

Clean Bean

Clean Bean specializes in making fresh organic tofu, using the best ingredients and traditional techniques and has been supplying us with tofu for over 12 years. You can find Clean Bean tofu at The Organic Delivery Company and Planet Organic (see below), both of which offer a great range of other organic fresh foods and dry goods.
www.cleanbean.co.uk

Cool Chile Co

For all your chilli needs – whole, crushed and in powder from. This is also where you can find Mexican oregano and epazote.
www.coolchile.co.uk

Forge Farm

Situated in rural Oxfordshire, we get the best selection of organic pumpkins and squash delivered to us every year from this family-run farm. Unfortunately Greg only offers his products to the wholesale market, but your local farmers' markets and greengrocers should have a good selection of pumpkin and squash when in season. If you can't find them and have the time and inclination you can buy the seeds directly from Forge Farm.
www.forgefarm.com

Holland & Barrett and Whole Foods Market

Both these stores have locations across the UK and have a great selection of products including gluten-free flours, vegetable bouillon powders, vegan margarine, agar agar, soy milk, soy cream and various other soy, gluten-free and vegan products, as well as a good selection of grains, beans and pulses.

At Whole Foods Market you can also find a great selection of organic and gluten-free breads, as well as heirloom varieties of fresh vegetables and vegetarian cheeses
www.hollandandbarrett.com
www.wholefoodsmarket.com

I Camisa & Son and Lina Stores

These two Italian delicatessens are local to us here in in Soho and have a great range of fresh pastas, some vegetarian cheeses, beans, pulses and various dry goods, as well as a selection of breads.
www.icamisa.co.uk
www.linastores.co.uk

Infinity Foods

If you're lucky enough to live in or around Brighton then you will know what an amazing selection of vegetarian products Infinity Foods has to offer, from organic grains, beans and pulses, bakery and local fresh produce and a great selection of grocery products. This co-operative has been supplying us with the bulk of our dry goods for well over 12 years and is a must visit whenever I'm in the local area.
www.infinityfoodsretail.co.uk

Jus-Rol

Their products include vegetarian and vegan puff pastry, both readily available at the following online stores:
www.waitrose.com
www.ocado.com
www.tesco.com

Naturescape

If your finding it hard to find wild garlic when in season at your local farmers' market or whole foods store, naturescape will deliver them to you for around £13 from the end of February until the middle of April. You can purchase 50 bulbs in the green and ready to use.
www.naturescape.co.uk

New Loon Moon and See Woo

These are two of the biggest and best Oriental supermarkets in London's Chinatown, with a vast range of Japanese, Chinese, Thai and Korean products. See Woo also has locations in Greenwich and in Glasgow. If these stores aren't in your local area try www.theasiancookshop.co.uk.
www.newloonmoon.com
www.seewoo.com

Odysea

Another long-standing supplier of all our traditional Greek and contemporary Mediterranean foodstuffs, with a great selection of products, including their own branded goods ready to order online. They have everything from good-quality olive oils, truffle-infused oil, feta and halloumi cheeses, olives, pita breads and so much more.
www.odysea.com

The Organic Delivery Company

Offers a fruit and veg box delivery service, as well as a wide range of ingredients, include dairy alternatives and superfoods.
www.organicdeliverycompany.co.uk

Ottolenghi

Has a great selection of Middle Eastern spices and really good-quality pomegranate molasses, rose water and rose petals, vine leaves and other various speciality ingredients.
www.ottolenghi.co.uk/pantry

Planet Organic

With several stores across London as well as a thriving online business, Planet Organic has a wide range of foods on offer, including gluten-free and dairy-free products.
www.planetorganic.com

INDEX

ACKNOWLEDGEMENTS

A massive thank you to Eleanor and Yasia from Octopus, and Dan and Sarah who between them took this from the back burner and brought it to a rolling boil.

To Jonathan, Patrick, Annie and Tabitha, whose photography, design and styling brought the Mildreds mojo to life.

To Martin, whose generosity and belief in Mildreds has kept us afloat when the chips were down.

To my three sons, Ambrose, Flinn and Milo, just because.

To Kathy, the absolute stalwart of Mildreds.

To everyone else behind the scenes whose creative talent has made this book happen.

And last but not the least, to Diane – we had the dream, Lambie.